Enthusiasts Guide
Honda Motorcycles

1959 - 1985

Doug Mitchel

Published by:
Wolfgang Publications Inc.
P.O. Box 223
Stillwater, MN 55082
www.wolfpub.com

Legals

First published in 2013 by Wolfgang Publications Inc.,
P.O. Box 223, Stillwater MN 55082

ISBN 13: 978-1-935828-85-3

Printed and bound in China.

Enthusiasts Guide Honda Motorcycles 1959 - 1985

Benly Touring 150: 1959-1966 — Page 6

CA77 Dream Touring: 1960-1969 — Page 8

CB77 Super Hawk: 1961-1968 — Page 10

CL72: 1962-1965 — Page 13

CA100: 1962-1970 — Page 16

CA110 Sport 50: 1962-1969 — Page 19

C105T, Trail 55: 1962-1963 — Page 21

C200 Touring: 1963-1966 — Page 23

S90 Super 90: 1964-1969 — Page 26

CL77: 1965-1968 — Page 29

S65 Sport 65: 1965-1969 — Page 32

CB160 Sport: 1965-1969 — Page 34

CB450: 1965-1968 — Page 37

CL175: 1968-1973 — Page 39

CB750K SOHC; 1969-1978 — Page 41

CT70: 1970-1982 — Page 46

CB350 K4: 1972-1973 — Page 49

CL350 1968-1973 — Page 51

CB350 Four: 1972-1974 — Page 54

CB360T: 1975-1976 — Page 56

CB200T: 1974-1976 — Page 59

CB550K: 1974-1978 — Page 61

CB550F Super Sport: 1975-1977 — Page 64

CB400F: 1975-1977 — Page 66

CB500T: 1975-1976 — Page 69

CB750F Super Sport SOHC 1975-1978 — Page 71

GL1000: 1975-1979 — Page 73

CM185 Twinstar: 1978-1979 — Page 76

CX500: 1978-1982 — Page 78

CM400E: 1980-1981 — Page 80

CM400A: 1979-1981 — Page 83

CB400 Hawk Hondamatic:1978 — Page 86

CBX: 1979-1982 — Page 89

CB750F: 1979-1982 — Page 94

CB650 Custom: 1980-1981 — Page 96

CB 900C: 1980-1982 — Page 99

GL500 Silver Wing: 1981-1982 — Page 102

CB900F: 1981-1982 — Page 104

MB5: 1982 — Page 107

VF750C Magna:1982-1983 — Page 109

CX500 and 650 Turbo: 1982-1983 — Page 111

VF750S Sabre: 1982-1983 — Page 115

CB1000C: 1983 — Page 117

CB1100F: 1983 — Page 119

VT500 Ascot: 1983-1984 — Page 122

VF750F Interceptor: 1983-1984 — Page 124

VF500F Interceptor: 1984-1986 — Page 126

CB700SC Nighthawk S: 1984-1986 — Page 129

Restorer Interview with R. Smith — Page 132

Where To Shop Parts — Page 134

Wolfgang Books — Page 142

Sources — Page 144

Dedication

I want to extend a hand of gratitude to Roger Smith and his wife Fran for his annual restoration projects and for being supportive throughout the years.

Acknowledgements

I want to extend my thanks to all the friends, associates and collectors who open up their garages to me when doing a new book. Without their willingness to allow me in to photograph their machines a book of this nature would never get done. I could fill most of this book with names of those who assisted me but to name a few will have to suffice. To the rest you know I appreciate your efforts and look forward to crossing your paths again one day.

In order of the alphabet, Richard Backus, Joe Bortz, Keith Campbell, John Davy, David Freeman, Ray Landy, Brad Powell, Steve Searles, Roger Smith and Buzz Walneck. To this gang of gentlemen and hooligans my thanks go out with a wish of continued prosperity and the collecting of shiny things.

Introduction

The reason for creating this book was fairly simple and we hope you are buying it for the same reason. With plans to buy and restore a Honda of your dreams, you may have some questions and within these pages we hope to answer as many as we can.

When I speak with my associate Roger Smith, we often return to the question of "where have all the Japanese motorcycles gone that were imported into this country in the last 55 years?" Considering the fact that tens of millions of them have been sent here, it's odd how few we see at shows, events and swap meets. Somewhere a guy has a barn chock full of the things but he's not ready to share. With no answer to that question we hope to be able to get a few more on your list checked off.

Before you decide on which Honda to select, we hope the information in this book will assist you in that decision. Odds are if you have a certain model on your lust list, it won't matter what we have to say, or anyone else. The heart wants what the heart wants and when it comes to getting a long lost motorcycle back into your life we understand that feeling.

With a little luck you can find both the cycle of your dreams and maybe some guidance in these pages. No matter how you go about your search and restoration we hope you enjoy the journey as much as your first test ride when the project is done.

Be well and have fun!

CA95 Benly Touring 150; 1959-1966

Honda first arrived on the shores of the USA in 1959 and began selling motorcycles unlike anything previously sold here. Stamped steel frames, tiny 49cc engines and styling that was unique all set the new brand apart. The CA95 Benly Touring was seen in two editions, labeled "early" and "late." I was not able to find the exact date that set the two periods apart, but a few cosmetic changes allow us to determine which was which.

The CA95 Benly Touring made its debut as a 1959 model and would be the seed from which many future models from Honda would sprout. The "early" versions were sold from 1959 to 1963 and can be identified by the following traits: The fuel tank bore a large chrome panel and small rubber knee pad. The rear fender braces were truncated when compared to the "late" editions, a smaller tail light, blackwall tires and flat sided mufflers were all ways to tell the period your CA95 was built.

The 1964 model seen here is a late model, and we can confirm that by comparing these traits to the early model. The chrome panels on the fuel tanks were now smaller with larger rubber knee pads. The rear fender brace is longer and carries an extra rectangular plate. The tail light is bigger, the bike rolls on whitewall tires and the mufflers are round. On both iterations of the CA95 we find a square headlight nacelle that carries an integrated speedometer. Four colors were available, black, scarlet red, white and blue were the choices and when selected were applied to the frame, fenders and side covers. There stylish Hondas came with spoke wheels and drum brakes at both ends and a 154cc parallel twin engine in between. A sin-

One of the earliest models sold by Honda in the USA, the CA95 Benly made for reliable transportation on a tight budget.

Displacing 154cc from a pair of parallel cylinders, the CA95 was fitted with only a single carb.

gle carb fed both cylinders and a 4-speed gearbox was included.

The early CA95 was built between 1959 and 1963 with the late version stepping in and lasting through 1966. Often called the "baby Dream" due to its similar appearance yet smaller engine. It shared the same frame as the CB92 but carried a bigger displacement engine in the frame. As time passed, Honda discovered many different methods of building motorcycles and the market soon saw a raft of new models in a variety of layouts.

Year-to-Year Changes

The only changes seen on the CA95 Benly Touring 150 was when they switched from early to late versions.

As stated above, changes made included a smaller chrome panel offset with a larger rubber knee pad on the tank. The tail light was smaller, tires were blackwall and the exhaust mufflers were of a flat-sided design. A shorter rear fender brace was another indicator that tells us which period in life the CA95 hailed from.

The late editions wore whitewall tires, mufflers with a rounded shape and a longer rear fender brace. Less chrome with more rubber on the knee pads were joined by a larger tail light assembly.

CA95 Benly Touring 150 Model Highlights

- Many early Hondas share major components which makes locating parts a bit easier.
- The CA95 used the same frame as the CB92 but you need to ensure the parts you locate are truly compatible before bolting them on and hitting the road.
- Basic assembly of the early machines was simple, allowing nearly anyone the luxury of being able to restore one.
- There seem to be fewer parts available online when compared to other models, but the age of the CA95 will have an

The square headlight nacelle was also used as the speedometer housing.

effect on that status.
- Assuming you are able to locate all of the required parts, assembling them isn't a difficult procedure.
- The 154cc engine is fed by only a single carb, making that aspect of the project a bit simpler.
- Surprisingly, much of the sheet metal components can be found online although as usual the exhaust remains a tough to locate item.

Specifications
Wheelbase: N/A Weight: 276 Pounds
Seat Height: N/A
Displacement: 154cc
Horsepower: 16.5@10,500 RPM
Final Drive: Chain (fully enclosed)
Fuel Delivery: (1) Carburetor
Fuel Capacity: N/A
Gearbox: 4-Speed Top Speed: N/A
MSRP: N/A
Production: 1959-1966

Motorcycle Ratings
Available Examples: 2 out of 7
Ease of Restoration: 4 out of 7
Replacement Part Availability:
3 out of 7
Final Value vs Restoration Cost:
3 out of 7

CA77 Dream Touring: 1960-1969

It seems like only moments after Honda came up with the 305cc engine they had numerous new models to power with it. There were more than six different iterations before the CA77 Dream Touring model came to be in 1960. The early editions ran from 1960 to 1963 when the late editions took over until 1969.

The clean design and easy-to-use features makes the CA77 an endearing model for almost anyone who rides.

The Dream was fitted with a seat cover that matched the color chosen for the body panels and was considered quite stylish.

The 305cc wet sump parallel twin engine was fed by a single carburetor, power ran through a four-speed gearbox. A drum brake was found on both wheels and with a weight of 372 pounds the binders did an adequate job of slowing down the Dream. The fact that it only produced 23 horsepower at 7500 RPM was another factor that made the drum brakes' job an easy one.

A set of medium-rise handlebars made the reach comfortable as did the ample padding in the two-person seat. A chain was on duty for the final drive, enclosed to keep stray lube from spraying onto the legs of the rider and passenger. A set of tapered exhaust tubes led away from the engine and wire wheels were still the standard form of the day.

You had a choice of four different hues for the CA77 Dream and they were straightforward. White, Black, Blue or Scarlet Red would be applied to every inch of sheet metal on the cycle, and the seat would often be finished in a vinyl that was color keyed to the chosen paint. As was typical for the period, a gleaming panel of chrome was applied to each side of the fuel tank which also sported a rubber knee pad. A single speedometer was housed within the headlight nacelle, mounted to be easy to read as the rider monitored his progress. The wheelbase of 51 inches gave the CA77 a nimble feel when on the open road, where it was capable of reaching a top speed of 90 miles per hour.

With all of the family-friendly features and easy-to-operate functions the price of $560 didn't seem out of line. Finding a clean copy in the world today is not impossible, but will require some focused efforts whether online or at swap meets, to be sure you bring home an example worthy of restoration.

Year-to-Year Changes

The only changes found were between the early copies 1960-1963, and the late models that ranged from 1964-1969. Even those alterations were minor and were primarily the contours of the fuel tank that set the two series apart. The same four hues were offered for the entire run as were the chrome side panels with rubber knee pads.

CA77 Dream Touring Model Highlights

The design of the parallel twin engine was easy to repair and keep running and even in today's market you can find a lot of the needed parts. The stamped steel body panels can be a little harder to find. If you can't find fresh examples you may have to brush up on your body working skills.

Whether it's engine or body parts, online searches reveal a vast array of available components to rebuild your CA77.

Upon completion you'll have a cycle that is worthy of almost any travel plans you have and certainly a great conversation starer around town.

Displacing 305cc and fed by a solitary carburetor the CA77 was easy to keep running and delivered good gas mileage.

Keeping the rider up to date on his progress a single instrument panel was mounted into the headlight nacelle for ease of use.

Specifications
Wheelbase: 51 in.
Weight: 372 Pounds
Seat Height: N/A
Displacement: 305cc
Gearbox: 4-Speed
Final Drive: Chain
Fuel Delivery: (1) Carburetor
Fuel Capacity: 2.6 Gallons
Horsepower: 23@7500 RPM
Top Speed: 90 MPH   MSRP:$560
Production: 1960-1969

Ratings
Available Examples: 3 out of 7
Ease of Restoration: 3 out of 7
Replacement Parts Availability:
4 out of 7
Final Value vs Restoration Cost:
4 out of 7

CB77 Super Hawk: 1961-1968

The design of the sporty CB77 made it popular with a wide range of riders and kept it in the showrooms for eight years.

Once Honda had created their 305cc parallel twin engine they chose to use it in a variety of models to suit different riders. The CA77 was the touring edition with relaxed ergonomics and added comforts. The CL77 was intended for on and off-road use and was labeled a Scrambler. The CB77 was the Super Hawk with sharp-edged sporting intentions.

The production of the CB77 ran from 1961 through 1968 which was a fact that speaks to the popularity of the machine. Carrying the same engine as its two other siblings didn't set the CB77 into new reaches of the performance world but the rest of the design was pointed in that direction. A

full 27.4 horsepower at 9000 RPM provided a top speed of 90 miles per hour. Weighing just under 400 pounds when gassed-up, the bulk of the CB wasn't an issue. A four-speed gearbox and a pair of 26mm Keihin carbs gave the pilot plenty of choices and precise fuel delivery on demand. A drum brake was found on each wheel and did an admirable job of slowing the CB77 down.

The 51 inch wheelbase combined stability with nimble handling, and when the tank was filled with 3.6 gallons of fuel you had a long day in the saddle ahead of you. Seat height was lower than some others at 30 inches which kept the center of gravity low, and allowed shorter riders to enjoy the CB.

Year-to-Year Changes

Within its nearly decade long run, we once again find early and late versions in the catalog. The only distinctions found between the two periods were in the height of the handlebars and exactly where the paint was applied to the front forks. Early copies were built with a set of flat handlebars and the lower sections of the front forks were finished in the bike's chosen color. Late versions came with low-rise bars and lower fork legs painted silver regardless of the color that was chosen for the rest of the CB. Listed options for the colors were black, white, scarlet red and blue, all of which came teamed with silver paint and chrome sides on the fuel tank. Period correct rubber knee pads were also included in the package.

No upgrades were made to the brakes, motor or chassis during the bike's eight year run.

CB77 Super Hawk Model Highlights

-    The sporty intentions of the Super Hawk were subtle but it became one of Honda's most popular choices with buyers

-    The CB77 was related closely to the CA77 and CL77 although each desig-

Capable of holding nearly 4 gallons of fuel the CB77 could run a long time when topped off.

Set into the top of the headlight nacelle are the two gauges, tachometer and speedometer.

A 305cc parallel twin engine powered the CB77 as it did the CL77 and CA77 of the same period.

nation was aimed at a different portion of the client base.

- The engine on the CB77 was a stressed member of the frame design, unlike the CL which had a sturdy down tube - perhaps to provide extra frame strength during those off-road excursions.

- Fully restored examples of the CB77 Super Hawk are currently listed at a few online sources with a wide disparity in the asking prices.

- Searching for replacement parts won't cause too much grief but won't come at a bargain price.

- I was able to locate copies of the exhaust in OEM trim and as expected they weren't an inexpensive option

- Owners of a restored CB77 Super Hawk will be pleased to find a capable and pleasant cycle in their hands and should justify the expense of returning it to stock trim.

Finished in one of the four color choices, this Blue CB is accented by the standard factory silver segments.

Specifications
Wheelbase: 51 in.   Weight: 398 Pounds
Seat Height: 30 in.
Displacement: 305cc
Gearbox: 4-Speed   Final Drive: Chain
Fuel Delivery: (2) 26mm Keihin
Carburetors Fuel Capacity: 3.6 Gallons
Horsepower: 27.4@9000 RPM
Top Speed: 90 MPH MSRP: $665
Production: 1961-1968

Motorcycle Ratings
Available Examples: 3 out of 7
Ease of Restoration: 4 out of 7
Replacement Parts Availability:
5 out of 7
Final Value vs Restoration Cost:
5 out of 7

CL72: 1962-1965

The CL72 for 1962 was the first of Honda's scramblers for the street and has grown to nearly cult status among collectors.

First offered as a 1962 model, the CL72 was Honda's first attempt at building a scrambler for the street. As we'll see with other machines in this category, the high-pipes, skid plate and bolstered handlebars are all the evidence of the bike's off-road capabilities. The chrome front fender hugs the street-tread tire up front and only a bit more clearance is found at the tail end. Unlike many Hondas of the period the CL72 features a frame that supports the motor, unlike others that use the engine as a stressed-member.

Powered by a 247cc, twin-cylinder engine the CL72 was a sprightly performer despite the fact that it was rated at only 24 horsepower at 9500 RPM. When dry, it weighed only 337 pounds and even filling the 2.8 gallon fuel tank didn't add much bulk. The electric start was deleted for this model, giving the rider a kick-start as the only way to get things rolling. The idea of course was a bike with less weight and minimal complexity.

The two exhaust pipes wrapped around the cylinders on the left and ran together above the crankcase to the back of the bike. Slotted heat shields to provided a modicum of protection to the rider and passenger. Despite the scrambler designation,

Setting this example apart from the rest is the alloy fuel tank of which only 113 were produced.

A large circular speedometer is the only instrument aboard helping the rider to keep tabs on performance.

With the creation of disc brakes several years away the CL72 is slowed by a drum brake at both ends.

street legal lighting was found at both ends, along with a chrome grab rail for the passenger for scrambling two-up.

Spoked wheels and a drum brake were pretty much standard for the day and fit well with the simple nature of the CL72. With a top speed of only 74 MPH one wonders just how much braking power the little Honda needed.

Choices between the three different colors were about the only options available and didn't change during its three year stint on the Honda team. Silver was the base color, topcoated with Blue, Scarlet Red or Black. A handful of only 113 alloy tank CL72s were produced which have become extremely collectible in today's market and will remain so since production of those gleaming tanks ceased in 1962.

Value for the CL72 tends to drift a bit higher than its CB77 sibling, but can still be found on heavily trafficked web sites across the world. The popularity of the original CL models means you are sure to find clean examples today - along with higher asking prices. The CL's ability to be used on and off road was a big draw in 1962 as it is today.

Year-to-Year Changes

Unlike most of the motorcycles Honda sold, no changes were made for the three year production of the CL72. Only when the larger CL77 came into view for 1965 did Honda make any changes to the popular CL format. Bumping displacement to 305cc brought some desired oomph to the light weight CL. The CL77 also had an upswept exhaust but was finished off with a small muffler that joined the two pipes together.

CL72 Model Highlights

- The ease of maintenance and readily available parts ranks the CL high on the list of desired classics from Honda.

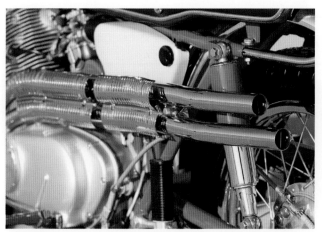

The twin high pipes were fitted with slotted, chrome heat shields for 1962

- The CL's design delivered light weight with adequate output and comfortable function which made it a top choice for buyers when new - and today.

- Being able to find nearly every piece of the CL72 on today's market makes it a relatively easy bike to restore and adds pleasure for anyone who wants to bring one back to its former glory.

- Finding one of the super-rare alloy tanks will more than likely drive you to distraction as only 113 were produced. The weight of the alloy tank is minimal but as expected you can dent or damage the skin of the rare storage vessel with little effort.

The twin cylinder motor displaced 247cc and was fed by a pair of Keihin carburetors.

Specifications
1962-1965 Honda CL72
Wheelbase: 52.4 in.
Weight: 337 pounds
Seat Height: N/A   Displacement: 247cc
Gearbox: 4-speed   Final Drive: Chain
Fuel Delivery: (2) Keihin 28mm
Fuel Capacity: 2.8 Gallons
Horsepower: 24@9500
Top Speed: 74 MPH

Production: 1962-1965

Motorcycle Ratings
Available Examples: 3 out of 7
Ease of Restoration: 3 out of 7
Replacement Parts Availability:
4 out of 7
Final Value vs Restoration Cost:
3 out of 7

CA100: 1962-1970

Built between 1962 and 1970, the CA100 (or Honda 50) was one of the best-selling machines in history.

In the history of motorcycling in the USA there may be no other machine credited with bringing more people to the showrooms than the Honda CA100. The simplicity of the step-through design and user-friendly controls put untold riders on the streets. "You meet the nicest people on a Honda," was the ad slogan of the day and may have been a bit of a stretch, but you sure did meet a lot of people riding the little Hondas.

Carrying a tiny 49cc, single-cylinder engine under its molded leg guard the CA100 only produced 4.5 horsepower but was capable of reaching 43 miles per hour. Preceded by the C100 and C102 Super

Cub models that first appeared in the USA in 1959, the CA100 was one of Honda's longest production runs during its infancy in the motorcycle world. Machines that are nearly identical are being assembled today and can be found roaming the streets of several overseas cities.

The C102 had the luxury of an electric starter while the other editions were kick start only. It was not much of a chore bringing the Honda 50 to life and it was happy to take you anywhere you needed to be while achieving somewhere near 200 miles per gallon. Price for the diminutive yet efficient machine was about $215 which made it highly affordable for nearly anyone who wanted to ride one home. Available in an all-white version or one of three other hues with white panels allowed you to maybe get one that wasn't an exact match to your neighbor's. Scarlet red, blue and black were the other options with no other choices were found on the order sheet.

The 50 had a compact wheelbase of 46.5 inches which made it very nimble and easy to handle regardless of your speed and physical prowess. A three-speed gearbox and automatic clutch removed manual shifting from the equation as well, making riding the 50 almost as easy as walking.

With most of the engine and transmission concealed behind sheet metal forms the 50 came to market with a tidy appearance - helping to fulfill Honda's desire to avoid the typical look of a full sized cycle. The 50 drew new faces to the dealerships in the '60s, riding one today still brings the rider the simple pleasure of riding.

The CA100 was designed and built to function at a high level while exhibiting many traits of a bigger motorcycle.

The single-cylinder engine of the CA100 displaced 49cc and delivered nearly 200 miles per gallon.

The molded cowl helped keep the rider's legs out of the elements - another of the many user-friendly features.

Even the handlebars were wrapped in sheet metal, housings to disguise the typical look of a motorcycle further adding to the bike's friendly nature.

Built between 1962 and 1970, the Honda 50 set many a young heart racing - and created an entire generation of motorcycle enthusiasts.

The gentle contours of the rear fender formed a subtle mud flap helping to keep water off the rider's back.

Year-to-Year Changes

Despite its nine years of production, no changes were made to the CA100 or "50" as it was also known. Its success did breed additional models from Honda and in those family trees we can find all sorts of variations. This one simply kept things simple.

CA100/50 Model Highlights

- Due to the lengthy production cycle of the CA100 models, parts remain at healthy levels on today's market.
- A current Ebay search returned more than 2500 individual auctions for parts and related materials.
- The easy access to every facet of the CA100 makes restoration an easier task than some machines that didn't gain such popularity in their day - there is an enormous amount of information available on the little Honda.
- The simple nature of the machine allows owners - perhaps less proficient in the mechanical arts - to tackle the task of restoring a Honda 50.
- Finding examples to begin a restoration can be found by heightening your search parameters on a wide range of relevant web sites.

Specifications
1962-1970 CA100
Wheelbase: 46.5 in.
Weight: 153 Pounds
Seat Height: N/A
Displacement: 49cc
Gearbox: 3-Speed Automatic Clutch
Final Drive: Chain
Fuel Delivery: (1) Keihin Carburetor
Fuel Capacity: N/A
Horsepower: 4.5@9500 RPM
Top Speed: 43 MPH
MSRP: $215
Production: 1962-1970

Motorcycle Ratings
Available Examples: 3 out of 7
Ease of Restoration: 5 out of 7
Replacement Parts Availability:
5 out of 7
Final Value vs Restoration Cost:
4 out of 7

CA110 Sport 50: 1962-1969

Honda's first foray into the American market was the introduction of their step-through Super Cub. Still being sold today they have racked up nearly 80 million units produced and sold. As time moved ahead they began to use the same formula and much of the hardware to create other new models for all the eager consumers in the USA.

The C110 Super Sports Cub made its debut in 1960 and while being nearly identical to the CA100 in mechanics, it looked more the part of a real motorcycle. It lacked the step-through configuration and had a fuel tank where bigger motorcycles had theirs, along with several additional details.

Following on the heels of that model, the CA110 Sport 50 was rolled out as a new model for 1962. For the most part, the new Sport 50 was the same as the previous edition, but included a few upgrades. The fuel tank was now fitted with chrome panels and retained the rubber knee pads that were common in the day.

The C110 had a seat long enough for two, just no place for the second rider to hold on. The CA110 by contrast came with a dual seat complete with a grab strap for a passenger. Early copies of the Sport 50 used the same 3-speed gearbox as on the C110 but after serial number 218192 they added a fourth gear. The chain drive was still enclosed to keep the rider and passenger safe from flying chain

lube. Like the C110, the exhaust was still mounted high on the chassis.

As with the previous model you had a choice of four colors. Scarlet red, white, black and blue were listed and would cover the frame, front fork and fenders. Both side covers were finished in off-white regardless of what color was been chosen for the rest.

The chain drive was fully enclosed to keep lube from soiling the rider's leg. Side covers have been modified on this example since Honda calls for off-white on all examples

Based on the super successful Super Cub the Sport 50 was a machine that looked more like an actual motorcycle.

Displacing 49cc and producing only 3.8 horsepower the CA110 was not going to win any races but could achieve more than 300 miles per gallon.

Although designed for street use only, the exhaust on the CA110 was mounted high on the chassis and came with a heat shield.

A simple drum brake was installed on both axles and the 49cc engine still had an aluminum cylinder head, as was seen on the C110. Weight when fueled was a paltry 180 pounds and that was part of the reason for the mileage rating of 343 miles per gallon.

By the time 1969 came into view, Honda had new plans for their next line of motorcycles, including much larger engines placed in machines that deserved to be called true motorcycles. Despite their small size and displacement, the C110 and CA110 Sport 50 played crucial roles in Honda's history and we should all be thankful as their design led to truly amazing things down the road.

Year-to-Year Changes

Despite its seven year production run the only alteration found during that run was the addition of the fourth gear beginning with serial number 218192. Beyond that nothing was altered on the Sport 50, though plenty of new machines were introduced to keep the buyers in the US customers happy.

CA110 Sport 50 Model Highlights

- As we've learned from other early Honda models, the availability of parts is a bit scarce.
- Much of the mechanics on the Sport 50 are common with the previous Super Cub, but care must be taken to ensure proper fitment.
- The 49cc engine is a simple design and doesn't include or require many parts to be rebuilt.
- Big shock, finding a replacement exhaust for a Honda of this age will cause true headaches.
- A recent online search located several components ready for purchase and use for the Sport 50.
- Overall the Sport 50 is another straightforward design from Honda that can be assembled without much grief assuming the parts can be located.
- Not an impossible find but locating more than one copy of the Sport 50 will be a task only for the brave.

Motorcycle Specifications
Wheelbase: 46.3 in. Weight: 180 Lbs.
Seat Height: N/A
Displacement: 49cc
Horsepower: 3.8@7000 RPM
Final Drive: Chain
Fuel Delivery: (1) Carburetor
Fuel Capacity: 1.06 Gallons
Gearbox: 3-Speed,
4-Speed at Serial # 218192
Top Speed: N/A
MSRP: N/A
Production: 1962-1969

C105T, Trail 55: 1962-1963

Honda first hung out their shingle in 1959 and concentrated on selling small, easy-to-use cycles powered by 49cc engines. Most were aimed towards the street rider but 1961 saw the introduction of the Trail 50. As with later Hondas in the CL series, the Trail models were designed to be ridden on and off paved surfaces. The same step-through layout was employed and a skid plate could be added for protection of the engine.

Using the success of the earlier Trail 50, Honda added a bit of displacement and created the Trail 55 for 1962. The single-cylinder motor now displaced 54cc versus the previous 49 and was still mated to a three-speed automatic gearbox. A chrome luggage rack was now standard along with a larger solo-saddle and added chrome trim. The C105T featured a low-swept exhaust tube that was also chrome. It was changed to a high-mount for the next iteration in 1963. A chrome fender was another feature found on later versions that protected the rider from debris flung off the front tire.

Both the street and off-road machines were fun and easy to ride even if you were a first-timer. No need to shift gears and light weight provided a stable and entertaining platform, all of which made for strong sales. Rolling on a set of tires with a bit of added tread allowed the Trail 55 to be ridden off-road but it was far from being worthy of

true dirt bike performance. Weighing less than 150 pounds was one aspect that made the Trail 55 so much fun to ride. The rated output of 5 horsepower meant it was safe for nearly anyone to ride when coupled to the automatic 3-speed gearbox.

Based on the earlier step-through models from Honda the Trail 55 was intended to provide added use when taken off road

The Trail 55 displaced a total of 54cc and increase of 5cc over the Trail 50 it replaced

The Trail 55 sported a low mounted exhaust for the 1962 and 1963 models.

The small badge located under the saddle tells you if the model is a 50 or later 55 version

---

Specifications
1962-1963 Honda C105T Trail 55
Wheelbase:46.5 in.   Weight: 143 pounds
Seat Height: N/A   Displacement: 54cc
Gearbox: 3-speed automatic
Final Drive: Chain
Fuel Delivery: Carburetor
Fuel Capacity: 0.8 gallon
Horsepower: 5@9500 RPM
Top Speed: 48 MPH (approx.)
MSRP: N/A   Production: 1962-1963

Motorcycle Ratings
Available Examples: 4 out of 7
Ease of Restoration: 5 out of 7
Replacement Parts Availability: 5 out of 7
Final Value vs Restoration Cost: 3 out of 7

Values of a finely restored Trail 55 will seldom be a deterrent even for the most frugal buyer. An online search for current prices will provide a wide range and as usual those are based on condition and correctness.

Year-to-Year Changes

In the two years the Trail 55 was built only a few changes were listed in Honda's materials. Regardless of years, you had your choice of scarlet red or yellow. White side covers offset the unit color. The chrome luggage rack was standard equipment on the Trail 55 where it had been an option for the Trail 50. The 1962s had a low-mounted exhaust while the 1963 models wore a high-mounted exhaust with a large heat shield.

C105T Trail 55 Highlights

- Plans to restore your Trail 55 doesn't pose as many challenges as one of Honda's more complex machines primarily due to the smaller quantity of parts needed to build a new one.

- A recent check of online sources listed almost every facet of the Trail 55 being sold in either new or used condition.

- Body work, engine and trim parts can all be located with relative ease and we can thank the high production numbers for that aspect of the equation.

- Even your choices of color will be easy to replicate because they are not metal flake or candy based, simply solid hues.

- Being nearly devoid of chrome also saves you time and money as there are fewer shiny bits to worry about.

- Upon completion your Trail 55 will be happy to take you anywhere you want to ride as long as freeways are avoided - this is a bike with a top speed of only 45 miles per hour.

C200 Touring: 1963-1966

This example of a C200 was found on Craigslist with an asking price that matched the condition.

In the infancy of Honda's historical run most of their machines were simple to ride and operate. Their motors were also small in size to avoid scaring away first time riders. Prior to the introduction of the C200 and CA200 models, Honda's cycles were powered by 49cc engines.

Appearing for the 1963 model year the new C200 models were powered by 86.7cc engines using a single-cylinder layout as before. The OHV design produced 6.5 horsepower at 8000 RPM and shifted through a four-speed gearbox. Kick starting was your only option and when tuned the CA200 came to life with little effort.

Simplicity and comfort were both domi-nant features on the tidy machine as witnessed by the easy-to-start process and ample two-person saddle. Suspension at both ends also delivered a stable ride and a single instrument was on hand to keep the rider informed of his or her speed. The drive chain was completely enclosed keeping the rider's and passenger's legs free of flying lubrication.

With a total weight of only 115 pounds with a gallon of fuel, the C200 was easy to handle regardless of speed or parking needs. A small drum brake was found at either end to deliver safe braking from the 51 MPH top speed.

The graceful contours of the C200 fender was indicative of the era and add a bit of style to design.

Mounted into the headlight nacelle was the speedometer, the only gauge the C200 carried.

A chrome and painted badge identifying the C200 as a Honda 90 was found on the front forks. The same designation was used on many Hondas of the period.

Despite the fact that the C200 was built for only 3 years, a wide range of parts can be found on today's market. Overseas vendors in Thailand and the UK carry nearly every possible component, whether large or small, to restore a C200 back to factory specs. Sadly, the value of even a pristine example may not exceed your cost of restoration so care should be taken before you begin. As a riding choice the C200 remains capable and fun to ride that will get you around town in style with little or no fear of break-downs.

Year-to-Year Changes

As with many of Honda's early models, the C200 received no annual alterations during its three years of production. The C200 was sold in your choice of white, black or red in the USA with blue being seen in Canada. The fact that no modifications were seen in any of the three production years means parts made for a 1963 will work on a 1966 and so on.

C200 Model Highlights

- The cost to acquire a complete C200 today has a narrow range but all appear to fall within a price point that makes them a great choice for a restoration project.

- Parts are readily available in several Thailand and UK based suppliers to fill nearly every need of the restorer at a fair price. This can't be said for every Honda found in this book.

- The lightweight and simple design of the C200 makes it a terrific starting point for even the beginner and will prove to be an enjoyable ride when the hard work of restoration is completed.

- A recent online search revealed multiple sources for parts - every part of the C200 is available at prices that seem very reasonable.

A hallmark of early Hondas were the front forks and the chasss, produced from steel stampings.

A single 87cc cylinder formed the heart of the C200 and provided enough power for a rider and passenger, as long as they weren't in a hurry.

The exhaust on this example is original and in really nice condition considering the age of the cycle and adds to the value of the machine prior to restoration.

Specifications
1963-1966 Honda C200
Wheelbase: 47 in.   Weight: 115 Lbs.
Seat Height: 30 in.
Displacement: 86.7cc
Gearbox: 4-speed   Final Drive: Chain
Fuel Delivery:
Keihin PW18HA Carburetor
Fuel Capacity: 1.9 Gallons
Horsepower: 6.5@8000 RPM
Top Speed: 51 MPH
MSRP: $ 189 (Approx.)
Production: 1963-1966

Motorcycle Ratings
Available Examples: 2 out of 7
Ease of Restoration: 4 out of 7
Replacement Parts Availability:
3 out of 7
Final Value vs Restoration Cost:
3 out of 7

The simple nature of the C200 provides a great plat-form for a restoration project especially when so many parts can still be located.

S90 Super 90: 1964-1969

In the first decade of Honda's presence in the USA the dealerships were filled with a variety of bikes powered by small engines. Eventually, however, Honda designed and built new engines with displacement nearly twice the size of the first glut of 49cc engines seen in the US.

For the 1964 model year Honda rolled out the S90, otherwise named the Super 90. Also sold in scrambler form the S90 was designed for street use only while the CL variant could travel over unpaved surfaces as well. The Super 90 was a diminutive choice for smaller or beginning riders and still provided a range of features usually found on larger cycles. A 4-speed gearbox was mated to the 89cc, single-cylinder engine that hung from the frame at a 75 degree angle. The solitary exhaust pipe hung low on the S90 whereas the CL edition had a high-pipe to avoid starting brush fires when riding off road. Weighing less than 200 pounds when fully topped off with fuel the Super 90 was easy to maneuver at speed or in the garage. The S90 was rated at 8 horsepower which was able to propel it to a top speed of 63 MPH.

A drum brake was found on either wheel along with spoked

Produced from 1964 to 1969 the S90 or Super 90 provided the owner with a great package of compact size and decent performance.

With 1.85 gallons of fuel aboard the S90 could travel a great distance due to its efficient design

rims. A saddle capable of carrying two adults was included along with a solitary speedometer integrated into the headlight nacelle. Suspension at both ends of the chassis delivered enough comfort whether carrying only the rider or a passenger. The graceful fuel tank, complete with period-correct knee pads and chrome sides could carry nearly two gallons of fuel. Your choice of four colors were found on the order sheet: white, black, scarlet red (for the early models), candy red (for later editions and candy blue also after March of 1968. The headlight nacelle and upper segments of the front forks were finished in the same color as that chosen for the tank, with a set of rubber gators covering the lower section of the front forks.

Year-to-Year Changes

During its 5 years of production scant alterations were seen and none pertained to the mechanical functions. S90s built prior to March of 1968 were delivered with front and rear fenders painted silver regardless of the selected unit color. Chrome plated units would be used on any examples built after March of 1968. Leading up to the 1968 models only standard paint could be chosen while candy tones were offered later in the run. Of those candy hues, red and blue

Integrated into the headlight nacelle is the only instrument found on the Super 90.

A well-padded saddle was included in the Sport 90's inventory of rider-friendly features.

Fed by a single Keihin 20mm carburetor, the single-cylinder engine displaced 89cc.

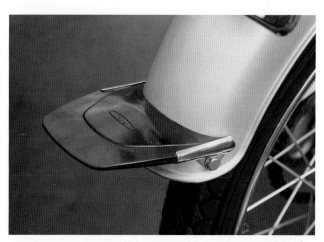

Attached to the rear fender was this rigid mud flap.

were on tap alongside the continuing black and white choices.

Super 90 Model Highlights

- A production run of five years put a large number of the S90s on the street, and finding clean copies today is not that tough.
- Finding replacement parts is likewise relatively easy using primarily online sources.
- Unlike many Hondas of the same period, finding a replacement for the original exhaust is not as difficult as you might expect.
- Having made no mechanical changes during the production allows you to mix and match parts for any of the years.
- When completed you'll have a great machine that is capable of scuttling you and a friend around town with no hesitation.
- Colors for the early models were not candy or metallic which creates an easier process of replacing with fresh paint.
- Equipped with only a kick-start lever eliminates one potential service issue regarding an electric starter and its woes.

The tail end of the Super 90 was suspended by a pair of shocks with no provision for adjustment.

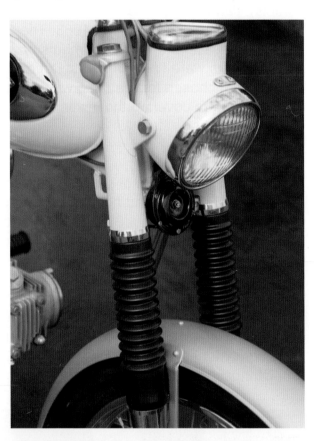

The headlight nacelle and upper fork tubes were finished in unit color with rubber gators covering the lower section of each fork leg.

Specifications	Production: 1964-1968
Wheelbase: 47 in. Weight: 179 Pounds	
Seat Height: N/A Displacement: 89cc	Motorcycle Ratings
Gearbox: 4-Speed Final Drive: Chain	Availability of examples: 3 out of 7
Fuel Delivery: (1) Keihin 20mm PW20H	Ease of Restoration: 3 out of 7
Fuel Capacity: 1.85 Gallons	Replacement Parts Availability:
Horsepower: 8@9500 RPM	4 out of 7
Top Speed: 63 MPH	Final Value vs Restoration:
MSRP: N/A	Cost 2 out of 7

CL77: 1965-1968

Features that allowed the CL77 to be ridden in many different conditions was one of its biggest attractions.

The Scrambler designation was assigned to those machines that were suited for both on and off-road riding. Once the term was coined a large number of motorcycles were designed to fall into the category. Most were better at off-road conditions than a true street machine but lacked the required features that could be found on a true off-road model.

Although labeled a "Trail" model one of Honda's earliest forays into the dual-purpose offerings was the C105T Trail sold in the USA in 1962-1963. The first editions of these still wore an exhaust that ran low on the chassis which flew in the face of the typical off road or scrambler application.

Shown on the Honda dockets for three years, the CL77 would become an iconic favorite among Honda riders and collectors. Making its debut as a 1965 model the CL77 delivered a great combination of features that could be used in many conditions and be ridden on the street or on the trails. The close-fitting fenders would hamper the CL77 in a truly rugged surface but would suffice under most off-pavement riding. The upswept exhaust was a true indicator of bike's intent and helped to prevent setting fires to the passing underbrush.

Other closely related family members were Honda's C77 Dream and CB77 Super Hawk models, evidence of the strength of

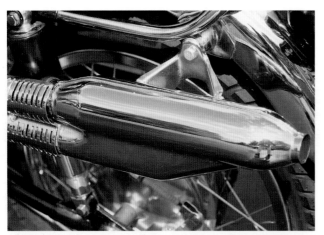

The pair of exhaust pipes merged into a single muffler at the end of their run - all in bright chrome plating.

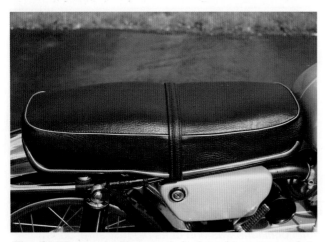

The CL77 came with a seat designed to accomodate two riders.

Nestled in the top of the headlight nacelle is the speedometer.

the family's bloodlines. The CL used a more substantial frame design that included a vertical down tube for added support. The bikes shared a powerplant and basic chassis geometry, although the CL wore 19 inch rims to better suit off the road travels. To shave a few pounds from the overall weight the CL was not fitted with an electric start. When fully loaded with fuel and the required fluids the CL77 still weighed in at under 400 pounds, which helped to make it nimble when riding on or off-road. One limiting factor may have been the 4-speed gearbox, but few complained as that was the standard of the day. A well-padded two-person saddle allowed a friend to ride along whether in town or in the open fields.

Drum brakes were found at both ends, but the 1966 and later editions were equipped with larger capacity binders borrowed from the larger CB450.

The CL77 has a large group of followers and restored examples can often be seen at a variety of shows and events around the country.

Year-to-Year Changes

During the multi-year production run only cosmetic changes were seen save the brake upgrade on the 1966 models. Within the four year model run the changes in colors and trim were only listed as "early" and "late" but no actual dates for this break could be located.

Early copies wore fenders painted in silver along with sheet metal offered in blue, red or black. Late examples wore chrome fenders with your choice of candy orange, candy blue or silver for the painted components. The late models also wore a frame and headlight bucket painted black regardless of the hue selected for the tank and side covers. The upswept exhaust with a single muffler was used on the entire production run and was finished in chrome. Early CL's featured a frame and headlight

The serpentine exhaust used on the CL kept the pipes high and out of harm's way when riding off road.

bucket of blue, red or black with fenders, tank and side covers finished in silver paint.

CL77 Model Highlights

-    A vast supply of replacement parts can be found for the CL series making it one of the easier machines to return to stock trim

-    The parallel-twin motor is of a straightforward design and assembly allowing for easy maintenance and upkeep.

Displacing 305cc, the parallel twin engine in the CL77 provided plenty of power and was easy to maintain.

-    Although the exhaust was chrome throughout the bike's production, only the fenders were chrome on late editions.

-    A choice of three colors were offered and early and late copies all of which are an easy match with today's paint options.

-    For 1966 and beyond the brakes on the CL77 were taken from the CB450 model which enhanced stopping power.

-    With only a change in braking the rest of the series can share parts with ease

-    A slightly bigger wheel diameter of 19 inches is one distinct dimension of the CL when compared to its rivals the CB and C77 models.

Specifications	MSRP: $707
Wheelbase: 52.4 in. Weight: 383 Pounds	Production: 1965-1968
Seat Height: 32.3 in.	
Displacement: 305.4 in.	Motorcycle Ratings
Gearbox: 4-Speed Final Drive: Chain	Available Examples: 3 out of 7
Fuel Delivery: (2) 26mm Keihin	Ease of Restoration: 4 out of 7
Carburetors	Replacement Parts Availability: 5 out of 7
Fuel Capacity: 3.7 Gallons	Final Value vs Restoration Cost:
Horsepower: 28.5@9000 RPM	5 out of 7
Top Speed: 85 MPH	

S65 Sport 65: 1965-1969

Built for four years, the Honda Sport 65 combined features of both their simpler bikes and the bigger, more capable machines.

Honda was still a young company in 1965, experimenting with several variations in their designs. Their step-through models were still bringing a new breed of rider to the showrooms. Once through the door and some of those sought more than a 49cc machine. Small displacement engines still ruled the roost when the Sport 65 came to be, but by the end of its production Honda would have released the grand-daddy of big bikes.

The Sport 65, or S65 as it was also named, combined several facets of design into a single cycle that promised a higher degree of performance and comfort than that offered by some of the smaller models.

The ad for the Sport 65 was titled, Hot New One From Honda, and spoke at length about what this latest model could do for the rider.

The 63cc engine was a single-cylinder layout mated to a 4-speed gearbox. Unlike some smaller models on the market, this transmission came with an old fashioned manual clutch. Weighing less than 200 pounds when fully fueled, the Sport 65 displayed a sprightly personality that added to the bike's appeal. The upswept exhaust allowed riding off the paved surfaces - despite the tire hugging fenders that would limit true off-road action. Rated at 6.2 horsepower at 10,000 RPM The bike's performance was on par for the period and proved adequate for riding two-up. the relatively large saddle, covered in a two-tone vinyl, helped to ensure that riding double would be as comfortable as possible. A stamped steel frame was par for the course for small bikes built during the period.

The S65 could reach a top speed of 56 miles per hour and sipped fuel from a 1.72 gallon tank. The painted, chrome and rubber knee pads were typical of the day as were the drum brakes at each end. The slotted heat shield that protected the rider's legs from the exhaust was another feature often seen on cycles that could be ridden off-road. Only three colors were offered and didn't change during the four year production of the S65. white, black and scarlet red were the choices offered allowing the buyer the opportunity to avoid having one just like his neighbor.

Year-to-Year Changes

Although the Sport 65 was produced for four years, there were no listed changes during any of those years. The simplistic nature of the design and great response from buyers told Honda to leave a good thing alone. They did however continue to expand their offerings in other segments of the market.

Sport 65 Model Highlights

-    Having a frame that was created using stamped steel provided Honda with a consistent method of construction that provided an adequate structure for this light motorcycle.
-    The mechanical operation of the S65 was also a straightforward affair which gives the buyer and restorer few challenges.

-    A decent number of parts, both minor and major, can be found at a variety of online sources.
-    Once the restoration is complete you'll be the owner of a fine machine from Honda's early days that can be ridden today.
-    The basic nature of the single-cylinder engine is another facet of the design that lends itself well to a restoration by even the most basic shade tree mechanic.
-    With a displacement of only 63cc you won't be setting any speed records but will enjoy a high miles-per-gallon experience while riding the S65.

Specifications
Wheelbase: 45.3 in.
Weight: 183 Pounds
Seat Height: N/A
Displacement: 63cc
Gearbox: 4-Speed
Final Drive: Chain
Fuel Delivery: Carburetor
Fuel Capacity: 1.72 Gallons
Horsepower: 6.2@10,000 RPM
Top Speed: 56 MPH
MSRP: N/A
Production: 1965-1969

Motorcycle Ratings
Available Examples: 2 out of 7
Ease of Restoration:
3 out of 7
Replacement Parts Availability:
3 out of 7
Final Value vs Restoration Cost:
3 out of 7

CB160 Sport: 1965-1969

The CB160 Sport used sheet metal that separated it from other models in the Honda catalog along with a higher power output engine.

Nestled amongst the related models from Honda of that era, the CB160 Sport had intentions of offering more performance with less luxury. Powered by the same 161cc parallel-twin engine as the CA160, the remaining hardware was altered to better suit the "sport" designation. In the latter part of the 1960s Honda found customers demanding more power and comfort from their motorcycles, and in keeping with those desires they were constantly upgrading previous models to satisfy the demands.

As a rule the existence of a CB160 Sport in today's market is fairly rare. Like so many Hondas of the day, they were used and discarded as the original buyers simply traded up to more advance rides. For this fact alone, the value of a fully restored CB160 Sport will more than likely lag behind any monies invested in bringing one back to its factory trim levels.

With a weight of only 294 pounds and a horsepower rating of 16.5, the CB160 was one of the models suited to a riders looking for more power. With a red-line of 10,000 RPM the little single cylinder Honda was a lively performer for the day. The tire-hugging front fender distinguished the Sport from the Touring models of the period as did the fuel tank design and several related bits of hardware. Black wall tires were used in place of the whitewall versions on the Touring editions. The CB160 Sport could be had in one of four colors during its five year production run and each hue was contrasted with silver fenders and side covers. Black, white, scarlet red and blue were listed as your choices. When selecting the blue body panel option you also got a saddle covered in matching vinyl while the other three hues had black seats. A solitary instrument was mounted within the headlight nacelle as was typical of the period.

Searching for fresh components to restore your own copy will be challenging as this model never carried any tremendous claims to power, handling or features. While being a terrific all-around mount it found itself surrounded by other machines that fell into the same category. Other motorcycle manufacturers of the period were producing highly competitive machines which simply added to the rapidly expanding field of motorcycles available to riders in the '60s.

Year-to-Year Changes

During the five years of production there were no alterations to the CB160 Sport. The same trim, colors choices and drive train were utilized in every example assembled. The fact that no changes were made once again opens the door for parts from any year fitting any other year produced. As stated above, the market for replacement parts seems to be a narrow selection regardless of vendor.

CB160 Sport Highlights

-    Among other models of the same period the CB160 held a minor performance edge due to the light weight and slightly higher output.
-    Sold in your choice of four different colors allowed you to ride home a machine that might differ from your neighbor's, helping to add a small degree of uniqueness to your own.
-    Cost for the first CB160 Sports was $530 USD which was neither high nor low when compared to other offerings of the day.

The solitary gauge on the CB160 Sport was easy to read even when reaching its top speed of 68 MPH.

Although using different contours, the chrome side panels and rubber knee pads were fairly typical of nearly all cycles produced for the period.

The flat, two-person, saddle on the CB160 provided both the rider and passenger with a comfy perch.

Tubular forks at the leading edge of the Sport were radically different from the sheet metal versions used on other Hondas of the same year.

Displacing 161cc from the parallel twin engine coupled to a pair of carbs delivered sprightly performance from the CB160 Sport.

- The two-person saddle was well padded and would provide adequate comfort for rider and passenger alike.

- Locating copies of the CB160 in any state of disrepair today is an uncommon sight.

- We were able to locate a few sources that can provide a degree of replacement parts but it appears as most of the sheet metal bits remained the least common.

- Since the CB shared a motor with the CA editions, components for that segment of the rebuild will be easier to trace and secure.

- On balance, spending the time and money to return a CB160 to factory specs will barely allow you to break even when comparing the final value versus the investment required to achieve a nice restoration.

Specifications
Wheelbase: 50.25 in. Weight: 294 Lbs.
Seat Height: 29 in.
Displacement: 161cc
Gearbox: 4-Speed
Final Drive: Chain
Fuel Delivery: (2) Keihin 22mm Carburetors
Fuel Capacity: 2.3 Gallons
Horsepower: 16.5@10,000 RPM Top Speed: 68 MPH   MSRP: $530
Production: 1965-1969

Motorcycle Ratings
Available Examples: 3 out of 7
Ease of Restoration: 4 out of 7
Replacement Parts Availability: 4 out of 7
Final Value vs Restoration Cost: 3 out of 7

CB450: 1965-1968

Making its debut for the 1965 model year, Honda's CB450 Super Sport was fitted with the biggest motor ever seen in their catalog. This latest engine was a parallel twin that displaced 444cc, the first from Honda to use dual-overhead-camshafts. The enhanced level of power earned the CB450 the nickname of Black Bomber.

Another unique trait for Honda at the time was the use dual, constant velocity, carburetors. A four-speed gearbox was included and did well transferring the 43 horsepower, achieved at 8500 RPM, to the rear wheel. A wet weight of 430 pounds made the CB450 a great performer, though the DOHC design got it banned from racing in the UK. A drum brake at both ends did an admirable job of slowing the CB450 and was typical hardware for the period. The combined tachometer and speedometer were enclosed within the upper portion of the headlight nacelle which made for an easy read when at speed.

The 4.2 gallon fuel tank was finished in black paint with chrome side panels. The black and chrome color scheme was the only one offered during the three year production run of the first CB450. A different version of the CB450 came to be for the 1968 model year, though it lost most of the Black Bomber's magic.

As a result of the truncated production, the Black Bombers still in existence are not a common find on the used cycle market today. The low build numbers also tend to drive the price beyond those of the latter versions of the CB450. It appears that if they come to market and are in great condition they sell faster than the 102 MPH top speed the machine is capable of. The unique contours of the sheet metal combined with the ready-to-please performance make the CB450 well worth the time and expense of adding one to your collection.

The Black Bomber was only produced for three years but remained unchanged during its tenure.

Both of the pertinent instruments were housed in the nacelle that kept the headlight pointing forward.

The 444cc engine was also fitted with dual overhead cams, a first for a production motorcycle and helped to boost the output of the early Honda.

A pair of fully functioning rear shocks added to the comfort factor of piloting the Black Bomber at any speed.

Year-to-Year Changes

The CB450 Black Bomber is one of only a few Hondas that had no variations during its lifetime. All three years saw the same black and chrome motif with no alterations in running gear, power plant or suspension. It ranked high on the performance ladder of the day and if taken to the streets today, very little disappointment will be experienced.

CB450 Highlights

- In light of the fact that the first CB450 was only produced for three years locating parts for any of the three can be used on any other built during the production run.

- A recent online search illustrated how many of the pieces can still be had at reasonable cost.

- The simple layout also allows a pleasant hunt for any needed replacement bits both stateside and overseas

- A recent online search allowed me to find all manner of rebuild parts, even those as trivial as carb rebuild kits and OEM hardware are available to restore your Black Bomber to its previous level of glory with a minimum of pain.

Specifications
Wheelbase: 53.2 in. Weight: 430 Lbs.
Seat Height: N/A   Displacement: 444cc
Gearbox: 4-speed   Final Drive: Chain
Fuel Delivery: (2) CV Carburetors
Fuel Capacity: 4.2 gallons
Horsepower: 43@8500 RPM
Top Speed: 102 MPH   MSRP: N/A
Production: 1965-1968

Motorcycle Ratings
Available Examples: 2 out of 7
Ease of Restoration: 3 out of 7
Replacement Parts Availability:
5 out of 7
Final Value vs Restoration Cost:
4 out of 7

CL175: 1968-1973

Like many of Honda models of the period, the CL175 was built for use in a variety of conditions.

In the early days of Honda's history we find a variety of models that are intended for one use but based on a machine with a different set of parameters. One repeated application of this formula is building a cycle for on and off-road use using the platform designed for street only riding.

The CL175 made its debut as a 1968 model and only a cursory review of its hardware tells us it is closely based on the CB175 of the same period. The CB wore an exhaust that was mounted low on the chassis while the CL carried a high pipe complete with heat shields to protect rider and nature from burns. The CL wore a front fender that hugged the tire which would dampen its ability for truly riding in treacher-ous terrain despite the exhaust's intentions and design. One exception to this rule was found on the 1969 models which used a high-mounted front fender.

In Honda's history we find CLs with a wide variety of displacements. Ranging from 50cc in the very early days to larger 305cc variants, Honda did its best to satisfy every rider and their needs. Every version of the CL series was fitted with lights and turn signals making them street legal, but the exhaust and more aggressive tread on the tires told us of the more flexible abilities.

During its six year production run most of the alterations were cosmetic in nature while the mechanical design remained near-ly untouched. The 174cc parallel-twin engine produced 19 horsepower and shifted through a 5-speed gearbox. Of course a chain provided the final drive and drum brakes on both wheels provided the rider with the means to stop. When fueled, the CL175 only weighed 302 pounds making it nimble whether on the pavement or a more natural riding surface. Though no one would call the 175 overpowered, the 19 horses would take it all the way to 80 miles per hour.

Year-to-Year Changes

As stated earlier, changes made to the CL175 were based on cosmetics with only minor alterations to the mechanical design in its six year run. The debut year was built with a tubular frame in a backbone configuration that allowed the engine to be tilted slightly forward. From 1969 to 1973 the frame was of a cradle design with a vertical downtube on the front of the chassis. This layout permitted the engine to be set at a more upright stance where it remained for the duration of the model run.

The 1970 CL175 had a heat shield on the muffler finished in black whereas chrome was used on the balance of production. The muffler shield was also seen wearing slots or circular openings during the 6 year run and was changed nearly every year.

The final year of production was 1973 and on machines of that year we find a tubular grab rail behind the seat and a pair of gauges that were tilted towards the rider at a more extreme angle, making them easier to read.

Colors were also changed every year as were tank graphics allowing collectors to tell one year from another with relative ease.

CL175 Model Highlights

-    A production run of six years provides a wide variety of available donor machines and parts for your restoration project.

-    Solid, nearly complete, examples can be found without a terrible amount of digging.

-    Prices for these decent starting points seem to be fair, if not downright inexpensive right now.

-    Replacement parts also seem to be available on a variety of online sources in both new and "as-found" condition.

-    Using a chassis layout that didn't change from 1969 to 1973 provides more part-swapping opportunities.

-    Paint and graphics changed every year so care will be needed to ensure the proper colors and trim are applied to the correct model year if accuracy is crucial.

-    Designed for use on and off-road the CL series provides the owner with a capable machine that's always fun to ride on a variety of surfaces.

Specifications
Wheelbase: 50.4"
Weight: 302 Pounds
Seat Height: 31.5"
Displacement: 174cc
Gearbox: 5-Speed
Final Drive: Chain
Fuel Delivery: (2) 20mm Keihin Carburetors
Fuel Capacity: 2.38 Gallons
Horsepower: 19@9500 RPM
Top Speed: 80 MPH   MSRP: N/A
Production: 1968-1973

Motorcycle Ratings
Available Examples: 3 out of 7
Ease of Restoration: 4 out of 7
Availability of Replacement Parts: 5 out of 7
Final Value vs Restoration Cost: 3 out of 7

CB750K SOHC; 1969-1978

I am willing to bet that anyone reading this book will have at one point in their lives wanted, or owned, one of these truly iconic machines. Making its debut as a 1969 model the CB750 instantly set the stage and raised the bar for what a motorcycle could be and did so at a decent price.

The inline, four-cylinder engine was transversely mounted in the frame and displaced 736cc. A bright chrome four-into-four exhaust led the spent fumes away from the single overhead cam (SOHC) engine - one that set new standards for smoothness and power. The four 28mm Keihin carburetors pulled filtered air through from the plastic airbox and filter, and fed that mixture of gas and air to the individual cylinders.

The big Honda's saddle could easily accommodate two people on long stretches of open road. The handlebars rose up to meet the rider's hands with no complication and were graced with user-friendly controls for lights, brake and clutch. Styling was basic (even staid by todays standards) yet the bike has become a classic.

The very first examples of this machine came with engine cases that were cast in sand. This technique was rather old school and labor intensive. Before the first year of production was com-

plete the casting was changed to a more modern method making the sandcast editions the rarest of the breed. The subtle texture of the motor gives away the sandcast designation and the value of these

The CB750 line was introduced as a new model for 1969 and was led by the now ultra-rare sandcast motor variety. The motors in these early offerings have become one of the hottest machines in the collector world as the numbers produced were few.

The side covers of the 1969 and early 1970 CB750s were the same but would be altered several times during the 10 years of production.

Early models used a headlight bucket painted the body color, while later models used a black bucket.

The side covers of the 1969 and early 1970 CB750s were the same but would be altered several times during the 10 years of production.

The contours of the fuel tank would remain the same for the entire CB750 series but colors and graphics changed with every model year. The first seen wore this simple stripe against a selection of vivid paint.

machines remains at the highest level today. The motor produced 67 horsepower at 8000RPM and sipped fuel from the 4.8 gallon tank. Tipping the scales at 499 pounds was fairly typical for the period and was the result of the steel frame as well as all of the related hardware. Even that weight couldn't hold the CB750 back from a top speed of 123 MPH. A wheelbase of 57.2 inches made the CB750 a comfortable ride at any speed albeit a bit of a handful in the parking lot. The seat height was also a bit tall at 31.5 inches making it a long reach for shorter riders.

The entire package was available at Honda dealers across the USA at an MSRP of $1495. Had we known then what we know now we'd all have brought home as many as we could squeeze into the garage.

The K model was the standard trim, an F or Super Sport edition rolled into view for the 1975 model year. The CB750F models wore different body panels including a sleek tail section and revised side panels. The engine remained the same 736cc inline-four but was fitted with a serpentine four-into-one exhaust. For 1977 and '78 the Super Sports also carried five-spoke aluminum Comstar wheels in place of the spoked versions used on the K models.

Year-to-year changes

Alterations made during the ten year run of the CB750K were minor. 1969 and early 1970 models found a four-into-one throttle installed and a headlight bucket that matched the selected body color. For late 1970 and 1971 K models a two-cable throttle was found along with smaller side covers that lacked the slots seen on the first editions. The 1972 K models wore headlight buckets molded in black with upper forks plated in chrome, replacing the color-matched tubes seen previously. Reflectors were also added to the tail light and frame. Except for the annual color options no other changes were found for the 1973 models.

For 1974 the speedometer wore a readout that was shown in the 20s. 1975 saw the readouts done in 10s and the faces of the gauges were dark green. 1976 saw the instruments finished with a light green hue. The side cover markings were altered for 1977 with the "750 Four K" seen in gold. The last year for the SOHC CB750 was 1978 and it wore side covers with "750 Four" graphics and a seat that was now stepped bringing the rider's feet closer to the pavement.

A range of colors were offered each year along with contrasting stripes to offset the hues. An insert of black was seen on the 1973-1976 paint schemes to further accent the chosen color and striping. Certain colors remain more distinctive as in the candy blue green on the 1969s, and Flake Sunrise Orange, 1972-1974. Every other year offered unique hues used only on that year with several variants of brown offered.

CB750 K Model Highlights

-     Except for the first year sandcast models, the cost to acquire a CB750 can range widely depending on condition, with many nice examples well within the range of nearly any budget. These were produced in fairly high numbers making existing examples easier to find than some of Honda's more limited production models. Care should be taken however, to ensure the example you find retains most of the original hardware as replacements for many items are getting hard to find at any cost.

-     Upon completion, the only significant value fluctuation will be found on the rare sandcast editions from 1969. These machines have commanded prices in the lower teens for years and finding remaining copies is getting no easier with the passage of time. The remaining models are so similar in design that there are no real standouts in the series. The 1978 will appeal to smaller riders due to the split-level saddle but they are otherwise identical to the earlier

One key factor is returning your CB750 to original condition is finding an accurate four-into-four exhaust system. They are getting harder to locate every year and costlier as their scarcity intensifies.

Five model years later the 1974 CB750 is mostly unchanged from its older siblings save for altered hues, tank graphics and side cover revisions.

One of the changes often found on the different years was a set of side covers that wore different badging and shapes.

editions in their mechanical configuration.

- The factory four-into-four exhaust is crucial to the value, but most machines found today either lack the system entirely or are in such poor condition they are of no consequence. Finding an OEM replacement is costly and getting more difficult to achieve with every passing year. There are some affordable four-into-one headers available on the market which work well at a higher volume but are far from an OEM clone.

- Assuming the machine has been cared for to any degree the motors tend to be useable and can be returned to factory

A black panel surrounded by gold and white accent stripes highlight the fuel tanks of the 1974 CB750 and the graphics tell you a lot about the year you are considering for purchase.

For the 1976 CB750 another set of color choices awaited you while no changes to the running gear were seen. 1978 would be the last year for the SOHC powered model.

specs with little effort. A large percentage of parts can still be found and purchased at a fair cost. The valve train can be adjusted using a feeler gauge and an open end wrench versus the layout of the DOHC models that appeared for 1979.

- Fuel tanks, side covers and seats are another consideration when undertaking your restoration. Most fuel tanks can be returned to stock with little effort although reproducing the paint can be costly if done well. Side covers are getting more difficult to locate but some aftermarket generics do a fine job of mimicking the originals at a fraction of the cost. As long as the seat retains the base in solid and undamaged condition you can get the remaining saddle recovered at many upholstery shops. Some slip covers can be found that are an easy alteration if the foam of the seat remains intact.

- Overall, the CB750 can be restored to museum quality as long as the factory paint and chrome are in good condition. Choosing to re-do either will set you back a tidy sum especially the chrome which cannot be done at home. Many of the facets required to restore your CB750 can be achieved with a competent mechanic and a selection of the required hardware, most of which can be found at swap meets or using online sources. As a rule, try to have all of the needed parts before you begin the process. As with many restorations you will encounter surprises once disassembly has begun but doing research in advance will keep even those events to a minimum.

- When completed you will find the first edition CB750 to be a comfortable and competent machine for the open road. Their overall size and weight may play a part at slow speeds but once up to speed on the highway you'll find them to be stable and entertaining partners.

*For the 1976 CB750 another
set of color choices awaited
you while no changes to the
running gear were seen. 1978
would be the last year for the
SOHC powered model.*

Specifications
Wheelbase: 57.2 in.
Weight: 499 pounds
Seat Height: 31.5 in.
Displacement: 736cc
Gearbox: 5-speed
Final Drive: Chain
Fuel Delivery: (4) Keihin 28mm
Carburetors
Fuel Capacity: 4.8 Gallons
Horsepower: 67@8000 RPM
Top Speed: 123 MPH
MSRP: $1495
Production: 1968-1978

Motorcycle Ratings
Available Examples: 5 out of 7
Ease of Restoration: 4 out of 7
Replacement Part Availability:
5 out of 7
Final Value vs Restoration Cost:
5 out of 7

*Another debut for the motorcycle world was the use of
a disc brake on the front wheel of the CB750 in 1969
and every year since.*

CT70: 1970-1982

The CT70 was also known as the Mini Trail 70, a bike that captured the imaginations of many small boys in the 1970s. That same lust has carried the popularity of the small cycle into the current time period. The design was intended for use on and off-road and could be placed into the trunk of a car for transport to the great outdoors - a process made easier by the bike's light weight of only 150 pounds, and the folding handlebars.

Built around a stamped-steel frame, the CT70 shared some of the technology seen on Honda's earliest machines. Introduced as a 1970 model the CT70 would remain in the Honda catalog through 1982 then return in 1991 for another three years of production. Changes were made on almost every new model year, but most were cosmetic only or an upgrade in features. On today's market you can find replica machines that hail from China. These clone bikes closely mimic the original CT70 and sell for a little over $1000 each. The Skyteam ST125 is one of many found on today's global marketplace.

This 1970 model is finished in candy sapphire blue which was one of three colors on the option sheet that year.

Candy ruby red is the chosen hue on this 1970 version and the simple layout is easy to see. Courtesy of LeMay Auto Group

The same 72cc, single-cylinder engine was used throughout the production run, always mated to a 3-speed gearbox that changed gears without a clutch. A total of five horsepower was on tap, enough to propel the CT70 to a top speed of 47 miles per hour. A tiny 19mm Keihin carburetor was aboard to provide the air-fuel mixture as needed. The exhaust was chrome plated on the early examples and came complete with a slotted heat shield that was also finished in chrome.

A well-padded saddle was part of the fun and could hold two adults as long as they were close friends. Front and rear wheels were a solid piece versus a spoked design, and both sported a small drum brake. The tires were wide with an aggressive tread for use on paved and unpaved surfaces. Their balloon nature also delivered a small amount of added comfort when traversing off-road surfaces. A simple chain drive delivered the power to the rear wheel without issue. Mounted inside the headlight bucket, a solitary instrument (the speedometer) told the rider the current speed.

Three colors were offered each year with the 1970 palette including candy ruby red, candy gold and candy sapphire blue with each hue glowing in its blended luster. A black stripe ran vertically around the center of the main frame section to offset your chosen color.

Year-to-Year Changes

The first group of CT70s ran for three years and was joined by the CT70H that had a four-speed gearbox and manual clutch. 1972-'73 versions had an upswept exhaust that was chrome with black insets. The speedometer was also a separate unit from the headlight unlike the debut versions. Each year would list different color options as well as modified labeling in both colors and design. Turn signals were added to the 1974 editions and would be included until 1994. From 1972 to 1994 the front fork was a different design, and for those sold from 1980 through 1982 a plastic front fender was seen in red to again match with the only hue offered. The 1979 versions had the downtubes of the frame removed along with the skid plate that had been found beneath. Steel fenders were painted yellow to match the only listed hue in that year. 1979 through 1982 also had a black exhaust system and heat shields.

When the CT70 returned in 1991 after nearly a decade of being away it was a close copy of the original models with only changes to colors and minor odds and ends.

CT70 Model Highlights

- In contrast to its diminutive size the production life of the CT70 has outlasted a large number of models sold by Honda.

- Between the enormous amount of parts available online and the latest Chinese versions being sold, adding a CT70 to your collection is an easy choice.

A displacement of 72cc was teamed with a 3-speed gearbox (for most models) with automatic shifting on the CT70. Courtesy of LeMay Auto Group

Wearing new stripes and features the 1977 CT70 remained true to the first editions. Courtesy of LeMay Auto Group

An all chrome exhaust and heat shield were used on the early versions with black being used as the years rolled ahead. Courtesy of LeMay Auto Group

The CT70 was a compact cycle that could still carry up to two adults. Courtesy of LeMay Auto Group

Black insets on the previously all chrome exhaust helped to differentiate later models from the first. Courtesy of LeMay Auto Group

- The versatility of the design has played a major role in its long life span.

- A recent check online found more than 8000 listings for CT70s and their related components.

- Selling prices for restored models today are quite a bit higher than when the CT70 was new, but more than 40 years have passed since it made its debut.

- The CT70 remains an easy machine to ride regardless of your skills, size or conditions.

- The simple nature of the original design has remained through all the later iterations, all part of the appeal for this little 72cc brute fo a bike.

- The open layout also allows a novice to restore a CT70 without experiencing much in the way of grief.

Specifications
Wheelbase: 40.7 in.
Weight: 153 Pounds
Seat Height: 28.5 in.
Displacement: 72cc
Gearbox: 3-Speed Automatic
Final Drive: Chain
Fuel Delivery: 19mm Keihin Carburetor
Fuel Capacity: .78 Gallon
Horsepower: 5@8000 RPM
Top Speed: 47 MPH MSRP: N/A
Production: 1970-1982, 1991-1994

Motorcycle Ratings
Available Examples: 4 out of 7
Ease of Restoration: 6 out of 7
Replacement Parts Availability: 6 out of 7
Final Value vs Restoration Cost: 5 out of 7

CB350 K4: 1972-1973

The two-cylinder CB350 Super Sport first appeared as a 1968 model and became an instant favorite among buyers. History tells us that it would be one of Honda's best sellers of all time even when compared to the CB750 released for 1969.

The design of the CB350 Super Sport evolved with each passing year and by 1972 it had reached the K4 designation. Honda typically started with a K0 moniker for the debut year then upped the digit until production ceased. The 1972-1973 version of the CB350 Super Sport included all of the latest features while retaining the original intent of the design. The smaller dimensions and use of the parallel twin engine gave riders plenty of power and comfort for the $735 entry fee. When topped off with all required liquids the machine still weighed less than 380 pounds, making it easy to move and nimble while riding on the open road. Rated at 32 horsepower the CB350 K4 could reach a terminal velocity of 102 miles per hour.

The engine, fed by a pair of 28mm Keihin carbs, displaced 325cc, and shifted through a 5-speed gearbox. Final drive was via chain, the typical format of the period. A drum brake at both ends provided adequate stopping power. A two-into-two exhaust was applied and was finished in chrome from end to end.

The styling was classic Honda with vivid paint and a simple reversed black stripe on the fuel tank. The capacity of

the tank could store 3.2 gallons of fuel and provided plenty of saddle time on a single fill-up. Four different hues were offered with the feature bike pictured done in candy gold. Light ruby red, candy bacchus olive and gentle maroon metallic were the others listed. The headlight bucket on this edition was black regardless of the chosen unit color.,

The combination of classic design, ease of operation, and adequate power made the CB350 Super Sport a top seller.

The 3.2 gallon fuel tank provided miles of pleasure aboard the K4.

The lower segments of the front forks were silver with the upper sections matching the chosen unit color.

A saddle capable of keeping a rider and passenger comfortable for miles was another factor in the high sales levels achieved for this model. A Scrambler version of the CB was also seen on the sales floor for those whose riding needs required some unpaved surfaces. The four-cylinder version of the CB350 made its debut as a 1972 model and quickly squashed the interest in the more docile twin.

Year-to-Year Changes

The K4 edition was sold in 1972 and 1973 and would be the final adaptation of the layout in 350cc form. Changes made since the machine's inception were largely cosmetic as the same engine, chassis and accoutrements remained throughout the production run.

Early versions wore two-tone paint on the fuel tanks with solid colors found on the side covers. The saddle on the 1968 models was finished with a non-pleated vinyl and would be the only year for that feature. A pleated seat cover and rectangular tail light lens appeared for 1969 and stayed the course.

On the K4s the "350" used on the side covers was enlarged, as was the tail light lens.

CB350 K4 Model Highlights

- When compared to other Hondas of the period, parts for the popular CB350 K4 are quite a bit harder to find.
- The basic design and layout of the K4 permits an easier restoration assuming you can locate the parts required.
- With restored examples a rare find, gauging prices is not as easy as with other machines of the day.
- The CB350G was similar but also sported a disc brake on the front wheel, was only sold as a 1973 model, and disappeared with the K4.
- With a pair of cylinders and matching carbs, getting the K4 to run well isn't a daunting task.
- As with most cycles built in the early 1970s. finding an OEM exhaust will remain your toughest challenge.

Specifications
Wheelbase: N/A   Weight: 375 Pounds
Seat Height: N/A
Displacement: 325cc
Horsepower: 32@10,000 RPM
Final Drive: Chain
Fuel Delivery: (2) 28mm Keihin Carburetors
Fuel Capacity: 3.2 Gallons
Gearbox: 5-Speed
Top Speed:102 MPH
MSRP: $735
Production: CB350 Super Sport 1968-1973, K4 1972-1973

Motorcycle Ratings
Available Examples: 2 out of 7
Ease of Restoration: 4 out of 7
Replacement Parts Availability: 2 out of 7
Final Value vs Restoration Cost: 3 out of 7

CL350 1968-1973

Honda built a number of motorcycles in the "Scrambler" format with many different engines. The CL 350 had one of the more prolific life spans with six years to its credit. The Scrambler designation told the world that your Honda could be ridden both on the street and off. About the only real difference on the CLs was the high-mounted exhaust system designed to avoid setting brush fires when taking to the trails. A set of braced handlebars and a skid plate beneath the motor also played into the off-road theme. Street tires and a close-fitting chrome fender over the front tire limit how much actual off road riding can be done but their intent was obvious.

Power for the CL350 series was derived through the parallel twin engine that displaced 325cc. A pair of CV carburetors delivered air and fuel to the cylinders and a five-speed gearbox provided the rider with all the ratios needed. Nearly the entire CL350 platform was shared with Honda's CB350 of the same period. The high pipes made the greatest distinction besides a different range of colors and graphics. A drum brake on each wheel delivered safe stops for this lightweight machine.

The Scrambler style gained a lot of attention in the day and remains a popular choice of many collectors. As with all Honda products the machines are well built and will run forever if treated well and maintained

properly. They are fairly light and provide nimble handling. The two-person saddle and ample suspension travel work together to provide hours of comfortable riding whether riding solo or two-up.

Values for the CL series has never rocketed north, but has stayed consistent when compared to other slices of the two-wheeled

The CL350 Scrambler first appeared as a 1968 model and was well received by the buying public. Shown is a 1971 model.

The parallel twin engine in the CL350 displaced 325cc and developed about 33 horsepower.

Changes to the side covers and badging are one of the ways to decipher what year CL350 you are looking at, along with tank graphics.

A drum brake was found at both ends of the CL350 which was adequate for a cycle of its size and power output.

universe. It appears that many parts, both major and cosmetic, can be found without a huge amount of digging. The relatively simple parallel twin engine is another facet of the program, one that ensures easier repairs when compared to the inline-four motors of the period. Reduced complexity of the entire design lends itself well to a person who may not be adept at major overhauls and complex mechanical repairs.

Year-to-Year Changes

About the only variations seen on the CL models built between 1968 and 1973 fall under the cosmetic column, the mechanicals remained constant. For 1968 and 1969 every example wore white paint on the lower section of the fuel tank and on the side covers. Your choices of available hues were seen on the upper portion of the tank. The upper segment of each fork leg was black on early production units with unit color being applied later in the process. Headlight shells on the 1968 and '69 editions were white along with matte black heat shields on the exhaust. For 1969 the seats wore pleated covers.

1970 ushered in a few more changes including the muffler heat shields in chrome; and the tank, side covers, headlight bucket and upper fork legs being unit color. A white stripe on the tank was used regardless of the unit color selected.

For 1971 a different configuration of the tank stripe was done in black and a trio of different colors was offered. The 1972 and early 1973 editions wore different paint in one of two choices. Upper fork legs are finished in chrome and the headlight bucket was black.

The 1973 models provided the passenger with a chrome grab rail at the rear of the saddle and the gauges were angled towards the rider's face for easier viewing. A white fuel tank stripe was used regardless of the chosen unit color and side cover emblems were black on white with "350" the only designation.

CL350 Model Highlights

- Simplicity of the design and execution remain hot spots of the CL350 family, with ease of operation and maintenance also scoring points of their own.

- Comfortable seating for a rider and passenger add popularity to the CL.

- The ease of locating OEM parts to replace those that have become damaged also leans the CL towards the positive column.

- Light weight and nimble handling make this twin a joy to ride whether on the open road or moving around a parking lot.

- The popularity of the CL350 when new means modern day riders are sure to find almost any parts needed to restore one of their own.

The saddle on the CL350 was fairly comfortable whether used on or off-road.

Specifications
1968-1973 Honda CL350
Wheelbase:52 in.
Weight: 346 pounds
Seat Height: 31 in.
Displacement: 325cc
Gearbox: 5-speed
Final Drive: Chain
Fuel Delivery: (2) Keihin Carburetors
Fuel Capacity: 2.4 gallons
Horsepower: 33@9500 RPM
Top Speed: 100 MPH
Production: 1968-1973

Motorcycle Ratings
Available Examples: 3 out of 7
Ease of Restoration: 4 out of 7
Replacement Parts Availability:4 of 7
Final Value vs
Restoration Cost: 3 out of 7

Wearing a top section that was painted to match the fuel tank a set of rubber gators were then finished off with silver segments at the lower end of the fork.

CB350 Four: 1972-1974

The debut of Honda's CB750 set a new bar for standards in the motorcycle market and the inline-four layout was soon to be attempted in a variety of displacements. The CB350 Four came in between the CB500 of 1971 and CB400 SS of 1975 and was deemed a fairly competent machine by period magazine reviews. First arriving for the 1972 model year the latest inline-four was a nice addition for those who sought a slightly smaller machine that could still perform. A comfortable saddle was also a nice place to spend the day whether riding alone or with a passenger.

A majority of the specs for the new model were typical of the day with a four cylinder engine fed by the same number of carbs and an equal figure used for the exhaust system. A five-speed gearbox was also a common choice for the period but despite the traditional technical details, the CB350 four outperformed the stats. When fully fueled the new model weighed in at a tad over 400 pounds which proved to be a reasonable load for the 34 horsepower on tap at 9500 RPM. Final drive was via chain and a top speed of 98 MPH was discovered during magazine tests. An MSRP of about $1100 was a nice entry point for a smaller machine that delivered such terrific numbers.

Produced for three years, the only alterations during that run were in the available colors along with stripes and graphics found on the side covers. In doing the research for this book I discovered a handful of the CB350s in perfect factory condition with no alterations from stock. Low mileage was another trait among the survivors and didn't seem to be priced as high as their condition might suggest. I am always baffled at how such a great machine can be left alone and not ridden during its lengthy period in owner's hands, but it's not the only thing that escapes my grasp.

The compact design and performance of the 347cc engine make the CB350 Four a great machine for the street

Using their successful inline-four layout, Honda created another winner with the release of the CB350 Four

The palettes of the early '1970s were getting a bit unusual for all manufacturers of cycles and cars and the candy bacchus olive used on the '72 and '73 versions of the CB350 Four is a perfect example. Not as bland as the Gold used on appliances, the yellow and white stripes offset the medium olive hue to a T.

Year-to-Year Changes

The first two years of production for the CB350 Four listed candy bacchus olive and flake matador red as your options for paint. Accenting your choice of base color were stripes of yellow and white on the fuel tank. Badging on the side covers consisted of "350 Four" finished in red and white for 1972 and '73. The final year of the CB350 Four listed only glory blue black metallic with tank stripes of gold. Badges on the side covers were dressed in orange and white.

CB350 Four Model Highlights

- Built for three years, examples of these compact four-cylinder models can still be found, many in really nice condition.

- A wide selection of motor, trim and chassis components also appear to be offered from a variety of online vendors.

- It's no shock that finding examples of the four-into-four exhaust will once again be your greatest challenge.

- The straightforward design and execution of this model allows the restoration process to be easier than others.

- Prices for even the perfectly preserved original copies have not yet climbed

Nearly every example of Honda's four-cylinder models came with a four-into-four exhaust that was quiet and hard to find on today's market.

Telling the world which model you rode was proclaimed by the "350 Four" badges on the side covers.

out of range and buying one in that condition will save you years of chasing parts and going through the restoration process.

- Interchangeability of parts between the three production years is another facet that brings pleasure to the search for replacements.

Specifications	Production: 1972-1974
Wheelbase: 53.2 in. Weight: 402 Pounds	
Seat Height: 31.25 in. Displacement: 347cc	Motorcycle Ratings
Gearbox: 5-Speed Final Drive: Chain	Available Examples: 3 out of 7
Fuel Delivery: (4) Keihin 20mm Carbs	Ease of Restoration: 5 out of 7
Fuel Capacity: 3.2 Gallons	Replacement Parts Availability: 4 out of 7
Horsepower: 34@9200 RPM	Final Value vs Restoration Cost:
Top Speed: 98 MPH MSRP: $1100	4 out of 7

CB360T: 1975-1976

The Honda catalog had a history of showing a model displacing 350-360cc for several years including some with 4-cylinder engines. The CB350G from 1973 was the most recent predecessor and that was followed by the CB360 in 1974. The 350 engine displaced 325cc while the bigger 360 edition claimed 356cc. Both used the parallel twin layout and shared many of the features. The 1974 CB360 was fitted with a drum brake on the front wheel where the CB360G carried a single disc. For 1975 and '76 we found the CB360T named in the line-up.

1975 was the first of two years the CB360T was produced. The T was a nicely equipped model.

The parallel twin engine design made maintenance simple, the bike needed very little maintenance.

The latest iteration of the 356cc parallel twin model still included a six-speed gearbox that was first seen on the 1974 CB360. The only real difference between the CB360G and CB360T was the last letter of the designation changing from G to T. Cosmetically the latest T model wore different stripes on the tank and a black cover over the points as well as a white and yellow CB360T badge on the side covers.

The engine produced 34 horsepower when turning at 9000 RPM and shifted through a six-speed gearbox. Weight was a sparse 391 pounds when fueled and the T could achieve a top speed of 102 MPH. The chrome exhaust was a two-into-two affair. One sorry note for the 1975 models was a recall to correct an issue with the engine and its cooling system. Government recalls were not as common as seen today so it is understood that the woes with the '75 T was serious enough to disrupt sales.

In the latter part of the 1976 model year the CB360T was seen alongside the

CJ360T. This new version was almost identical but carried only five speeds in its gearbox. A drum brake replaced the previous disc on the front wheel and a two-into-one exhaust was a new feature.

The appearance of the CB400F for 1975 was the death knell for the twin-cylinder models as the new Super Sport was equipped with added power and features that the T could not compete with.

Year-to-Year Changes

Produced for only two years the CB360T wasn't around long enough to receive many updates and nothing mechanical was a part of that plan. Paint options for the 1975s were candy riviera blue metallic or light ruby red, both with the same black and white accent stripes on the tank. The points cover was also black for 1975. For 1976 you had a choice of candy sapphire blue or candy ruby red. The points cover was now silver and the tank stripes were simpler and far less bold.

CB360T Model Highlights

- Although only produced for two years, examples of the CB360T are available on today's market.
- The cooling issues on the 1975 models was corrected on most of the machines

Displacing 356cc and fed by a pair of Keihin carbs, the engine produced 34 horsepower.

Graphics on the 1975 version of the CB360T were more visual than those used on the next year of production.

that were sold prior, but take time to be sure the one you locate has received the recall.

-   The simplicity of the parallel-twin design makes the CB360T an appealing option for those with more interest in riding than in tuning and repairing.

-   Despite the added complexity of the inline four cylinder design buyers flocked to the latest models equipped with such a simple power train.

-   Spoke wheels on the T models mean you may need to spring for new chrome if your example has been neglected in an outdoor storage as replacement wheels are not a common item.

-   The exhaust is also a simple design but as with most is not readily available in OEM form.

-   It appears that there are numerous options to replace many of the parts needed online, providing you an efficient method of tracking down the required hardware.

Specifications
Wheelbase: N/A
Weight: 392 Pounds
Seat Height: N/A
Displacement: 356cc
Gearbox: 6-Speed
Final Drive: Chain
Fuel Delivery: (2) Keihin Carburetors
Fuel Capacity: 2.91 Gallons
Horsepower: 34@9000 RPM
Top Speed: 102 MPH
MSRP: N/A
Production: 1975-1976

Motorcycle Ratings
Available Examples
2 out of 7
Ease of Restoration:
3 out of 7
Replacement Parts Availability:
4 out of 7
Final Value vs Restoration Cost:
2 out of 7

The disc brake on the front wheel delivered better stopping than a drum.

Standard fare for Honda in the day - the two large gauges flank a small array of warning lights.

CB200T: 1974-1976

During the years when Honda was creating a wide array of cycles powered by their inline four cylinder machines, others powered by smaller engines continued to appear. Based on the previous CB175 series, the CB200T was introduced as a 1974 model to extend the reach of smaller cycles.

Powered by a 198cc, parallel twin engine that produced a mere 17 horsepower the CB200T was intended for riders who were seeking transportation that didn't include highway travel. A top speed of 77 MPH wasn't too bad for the diminutive cycle, but the bike was better used on city streets and jaunts around the neighborhood. A two-person saddle was part of the design and worked well as long as neither of the mounted riders was in a hurry.

A weight of only 291 pounds and a seat height of 30.7 inches meant smaller riders could easily handle the CB200T and the asking price when new was only $815 in U.S. dollars making it affordable to almost anyone.

The angular lines of the fuel tank and side covers added some unique attributes as did the rubber panel that ran the length of the top of the fuel tank. A capacity of 2.4 gallons served it well as it was capable of achieving a high MPG rating. A cable-operated disc brake on the front wheel and a drum on the rear provided plenty of slowing power for this compact entry in Honda's catalog.

A CL200 Scrambler model was also offered for 1974 but was not seen beyond its maiden year of production. The CB200T was available for three years ending in 1976. For 1980 a CM200T Twinstar made its debut keeping the blood line of petite cycles alive.

Displacing 198cc and fed by a pair of 20mm carbs the CB200T was efficient while providing fun.

The CB200T was a compact cycle that offered the rider enough power to have fun but not quite enough for highway use.

Year-to-Year Changes

Only cosmetics and colors were changed with each year of production of the CB200T. For 1974 tahitian red and muscat green metallic were your options with "CB200" on the side covers in white. 1975 saw candy gold metallic or custom silver metallic as your choices and the side covers were finished in the same hue as the fuel tank. 1976 listed parakeet yellow and shiny orange as your tank color selections accented by black side covers.

No mechanical alterations were found during the three year production run.

At the rear, the little Honda used a very conventional drum brake.

While at the front the bike was equipped with an unusual cable-operated disc brake.

CB200T Model Highlights

-    Online sources for replacement parts are not as common as with others in the Honda family.

-    The value of a fully restored CB200T will probably not allow you to gain any monetary profit unless you bought the donor bike for a song.

-    Even the simple two-into-two exhaust is a difficult piece to replace as production of the CB200T never reached any great volume.

-    Collectability of the CB200T will remain about as low as the value due to the fact that the machine, even when new, was not considered a model that outperformed anything else.

-    Still a great bike for around town jaunts. but chosen as an investment will deliver only disappoint.

-    For those with an interest in the Café Racer craze the CB200T makes a great base for your project.

Specifications
Wheelbase: 50.8 in.   Weight: 291 Lbs.
Seat Height: 30.7 in.
Displacement: 198cc
Gearbox: 5-Speed   Final Drive: Chain
Fuel Delivery: (2) 20mm Keihin Carbs
Fuel Capacity: 2.4 Gallons
Horsepower: 17@9000 RPM
Top Speed: 77 MPH
MSRP: $815
Production: 1974-1976

Motorcycle Ratings
Available Examples: 3 out of 7
Ease of Restoration: 3 out of 7
Replacement Parts Availability:
    2 out of 7
Final Value vs Restoration Cost:
    2 out of 7

CB550K: 1974-1978

Like its bigger brother, the CB750, the CB550 was designed to retain the classic lines in a slightly smaller package.

The success of their CB750, debuted in 1969, led Honda to create several additional machines powered by an inline four cylinder engine. 1974 saw the introduction of the CB550-4 and much of the design mimicked the previous entry. Comfortable seating for rider and passenger, four-into-four exhaust and the SOHC layout kept the 550 entrant a close second to the 750.

All of Honda's inline-four engines delivered plenty of power with smooth operation in any gear. A five-speed gearbox provided the rider with enough ratios to fit any condition. When fueled the CB550 tipped the scales at only 454 pounds allowing the 38 horsepower to do an adequate job of mov-

ing the midsize machine. A set of four 22mm Keihin carburetors doled out the fuel at a precise flow to each of the cylinders. 3.7 gallons of fuel could be stored in the iconic Honda fuel tank. Actual displacement was 544cc with a chain for the final drive. Slowing the CB550 down was the responsibility of the drum brake on the back wheel and a single disc brake up front.

The handlebars rose to meet the rider's hands with ease and the rest of the hand controls were positioned for comfort and painless use. A small bank of warning lights joined the pair of circular gauges and the layout and graphics delivered easy to use control of the activity. Magazine reviews of

The dark green face of the instruments was changed to light green on the 1976 versions.

A single front disc brake was joined by a drum at the rear, together they did a fine job of slowing the CB550.

From 1974 until 1976 the CB550 exhaust saw these tapered, reverse cones at the end of each pipe.

the day spoke highly of the CB550's handling, performance and ride. The MSRP was listed at $1600 or about $105 more than the CB750s debut price.

Nice examples of the CB550K can be found today and typically make a great project bike. The primary issue will be finding exhaust parts, but that can be said for nearly any motorcycle of the period. Parts are readily available for many of the other needs of an older Honda and most won't break the bank. Prices for fully restored 550s are consistent unless you stumble over the person who has deemed his a rare gem. With no sand cast versions of the motor or special editions to raise the price even a perfect CB550 will stay within an affordable range.

Following in the tire tracks of the CB750K the CB550 was also offered as an F model or Super Sport. Sold from 1975 through 1977 the F model featured a four-into-one exhaust and different graphics but was primarily the same powertrain as was found on the K models. The F models were built for fewer years and in lower numbers making them a bit harder to find today and the four-into-one exhaust system will once again be a challenge to find and an expensive item to buy, if you do find one.

Year-to-Year Changes

Following in the path left by its bigger sibling the CB550K was little changed during its years of production. With the exception of available colors and altered tank striping there were no major changes made. The seat was altered to provide a split level stance putting the rider's boots closer to the pavement. The 1976 edition wore gauges with light green color in place of the darker hue seen before.

The tips of the exhaust canisters were changed for the 1977 and 1978 models. Early examples saw a tapered, reverse cone at the end of each pipe while the later versions simply featured a beveled end on every tube.

CB550 K Model Highlights

- The condition of your starting point will determine the cost for your restoration and I have seen numerous examples of these Hondas in a condition that was still within the realm of correction and none seemed to be over priced.

- Finding a factory exhaust remains the biggest challenge when restoring a vintage Honda and the CB550 is no different. Outlets that function as a supplier for those components are few and far between with OEM inventory almost non-existent.

- There aren't any drastic changes within the production range to set any CB550 apart from the crowd unless you are fortunate enough to find a super low mile copy with factory exhaust. Then it's not the machine that raises the value but the equipment still in place.

- Sheet metal, seats and side covers are also sore spots when buying used or searching for replacements.

- The CB550s were never fitted with Honda's Comstar wheels so spoked rims are all you need. These can be re-done without much cost with replacement spokes easy to locate. There are some aftermarket rims being sold in the event your factory hoops are too far gone to repair. Purists may find fault at the use of non OEM rims, but they will provide you with a gleaming replacement and a safe ride.

Fed by four Keihin carburetors, the CB550's inline four displaced 544cc.

- Once restored, the CB550 will prove to be a dependable and entertaining ride. The lower weight and diminished size as compared to the 750 mean it's a little more nimble yet still offers good performance.

Specifications	Production: 1974-1978
Wheelbase: 55.3 in. Weight: 454 pounds	
Seat Height: 30.5 in. Displacement: 544cc	Motorcycle Ratings
Gearbox: 5-speed Final Drive: Chain	Available Examples: 4 out of 7
Fuel Delivery: (4) Keihin 22mm Carbs	Ease of Restoration: 4 out of 7
Fuel Capacity: 3.7 gallons	Replacement Parts Availability: 4 out of 7
Horsepower: 37.8@8000	Final Value vs Restoration: 5 out of 7
Top Speed: 100MPH	

CB550F Super Sport: 1975-1977

Just as Honda did with their 750 series, the 550 models were sold in K and F trim, the F being dubbed the Super Sport. The basic running gear was the same between each of the two variations but the F were dressed in different garb and breathed into a four-into-one exhaust system that was plated in chrome. By using an exhaust of

The unique contours of the Super Sport exhaust are unique and difficult to find as an OEM component.

that design a few pounds were trimmed from the total weight and a sportier look was achieved. Graphics on the SS models was also different than on the K models, also with a sporty nature in mind.

The inline-four engine displaced 544cc and was fed by a set of four, Keihin 22mm carbs. A five-speed gearbox was on tap to deliver the 50 horsepower smoothly to the rear wheel. A top speed of about 114 miles per hour was available for those seeking added adventure. A concise wheelbase of 55.3 inches dispersed the wet weight of 454 pounds evenly and the seat height was 32.3 inches above the pavement. Final drive was via chain and the fuel tank could hold 4.5 gallons when topped off. The front wheel was graced with a solo disc brake while the tail end carried a single drum.

Having owned one of these myself I can attest to its ease of handling and manageable size. It is one of several I wish I'd have held on to instead of churning it for something else. Hind sight as they say is 20-20. Prices for examples found today have yet to reach any stellar peaks but tend to bring a bit more than the K models of the same era. Fewer of the Fs were manufactured so it only stands to reason that they would command a few more dollars based on their more limited production. Wire wheels were used on the entire series and cosmetic alterations are all you have to tell one year from the other. Produced from 1975 to 1977 the Super Sports were seen for two years less than the CB550K models.

Year-to-Year Changes

Only minor revisions can be seen for each year the F models

With the exhaust exiting on the opposite side, the profile of the F series is free of clutter on the left.

were built and they are primarily in the hues offered. The debut year of 1975 saw candy sapphire blue and flake sunrise orange on the tank and side covers with no accent stripes. the faces of the instruments were dark green and black rubber fork gators were seen on the 1975 and '76 versions.

The 1976 colors were flake sapphire blue or shiny orange, again with no stripes or graphics. the saddle was covered in dark brown vinyl and the gauge faces were finished in light green.

The final year of sale listed candy sword blue or candy presto red, both with a wide, gold accent stripe on the fuel tank. The seat

was again black and the rubber fork gators were removed. The faces of the gauges were finished in dark blue.

CB550F Model Highlights

- Remaining examples of the Super Sport editions are not as common as the K models based on the fact that they were only sold for three of the five years the K was available.

- Many parts for the inline-four models from Honda can be found on a myriad of websites.

- The serpentine four-into-one exhaust will again be a sore spot in your shopping efforts as copies are few and far between.

- Sheet metal and plastic side covers can be found but will require a higher level of patience and skills to locate.

- Replacement stripes for the 1977 models can be found at a source in Canada whose reputation for supplying such items is legendary (check the Sources Section).

- Locating the correct seat or seat cover for the 1976 model will be another irritation due to the brown coloration and rarity of the OEM production.

The Super Sport editions were a tidy package based on the sibling K series and were easy to identify with the four-into-one exhaust.

A solitary disc brake on the front wheel was mated to a drum at the rear and was adequate for slowing the F models.

Specifications
Wheelbase: 55.3 in.
Weight: 454 Pounds
Seat Height: 31.7 in.
Displacement: 544cc
Gearbox: 5-Speed Final Drive: Chain
Fuel Delivery: (4) Keihin 22mm Carbs
Fuel Capacity: 4.5 Gallons
Horsepower: 50@8000 RPM
Top Speed: 114 MPH   MSRP:$1730
Production: 1975-1977

Motorcycle Ratings
Available Examples: 2 out of 7
Ease of Restoration: 4 out of 7
Replacement Parts Availability:
     4 out of 7
Final Value vs Restoration Cost:
     4 out of 7

CB400F: 1975-1977

The profile of the CB400F didn't change for the three years of the production run, and that profile still looks great today.

Only six years separate the introduction of the legendary Honda CB750, and the debut of another four cylinder Honda.

Following in the tire tracks of the CB350 Four the CB400F was first sold as a 1975 model. The latest version of Honda's four-cylinder family was fitted with a 408cc engine and weighed a scant 383 pounds. The most unique feature was the twisted four-into-one exhaust finished in gleaming chrome. A six-speed gearbox was another feature not found on many machines of the day and did nothing to dispel the sporting nature of the new model.

Produced for only three years the CB400F experienced very little in changes during the three years of production. The design was heralded as being near perfect by reviews of the day as editors found the balance of power and handling almost without fault. With 37 horses on tap the CB400F was a spirited performer. A single disc brake on the front wheel was joined by a drum at the rear and provided plenty of power to slow the CB400F down.

Like a few other models in Honda's history the CB400F has taken on almost legendary status and is desired by many collectors today. Keeping that in mind, average prices have yet to begin an atmospheric climb with many examples available at a reasonable cost. As with nearly every vintage cycle certain components are virtually impossible to find if your goal is to return your example to factory specifications. The serpentine exhaust of the CB400F is one of the hardest items to find and if located be prepared to open your wallet wide. Future values of this model should be safe from falling but may not reach the levels of others from the same period. Finding an example that was finished in the factory shade of varnish blue will enhance value to a small degree but may not be worth the extra time spent tracking one down.

Overall the CB400F from the 1970s makes a terrific cycle for lively rides but may not be the investment piece you seek. If nothing else it's more fun to look at than a stock certificate.

Year-to-Year Changes

With the exception of available colors and a few minor alterations to the 1977 edition you'll find no changes between years.

1975 and 1977 models have side covers that are delivered in the same color as on the fuel tank. For 1976 the side covers are black regardless of which hue is selected. The 1975 CB400F was sold in either light ruby red or varnish blue, neither came with accent stripes. 1976 listed light ruby red again along with parakeet yellow and both choices wore no striping. The 1977 example was sold in candy antares red with gold and orange tank stripes or parakeet yellow with black and red stripes on the tank.

The 1977 models also came with a set of taller handlebars and a recessed cap on the fuel tank.

Regardless of the model year the CB400F was fitted with the same four-into-one exhaust system.

CB400F Highlights

- Never built in huge quantities the CB400F has grown to nearly cult status on today's market but prices have yet to join the climb.

Unadorned with any stripes for the first two years of production, the fuel tank held 3.7 gallons.

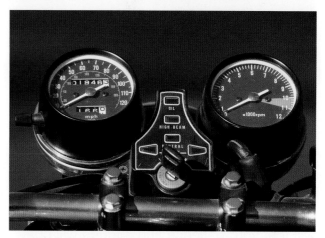

Typical for Hondas of the period the gauges are round, cleanly marked and easy to read.

For 1977 the handlebars were a little taller and the fuel cap was recessed into the tank.

The serpentine four-into-one exhaust was a staple on the CB400F for its entire three year run.

The 1977 editions were trimmed with accent stripes on the tank and the colors were dependent of the hue chosen for the unit.

1975 and 1977 models had side covers that mimic the fuel tank hue while the 1976 models had black covers.

- Replacement parts are not impossible to locate and many OEM pieces are sold online.

- Locating a correct exhaust system will test your patience and if found will challenge many check book.

- Having proven itself as a nimble and quick machine you will more than likely be surprised at how great it is to ride.

- Controls are typical for Honda and are easy to use no matter what skill level you possess.

- Electric or kick starting is up to the rider and the condition of the battery but it's nice to have the manual option in a pinch.

Specifications	Production: 1975-1977
Wheelbase: 53.3 in. Weight: 393 Pounds	
Seat Height: 30.7 in.	Motorcycle Ratings
Displacement: 408cc	Available Examples: 5 out of 7
Gearbox: 6-Speed Final Drive: Chain	Ease of Restoration: 4 out of 7
Fuel Delivery: (4) 20mm Keihin Carbs	Replacement Parts Availability:
Fuel Capacity: 3.7 Gallons	3 out of 7
Horsepower: 37@8500 RPM	Final Value vs Restoration Cost:
Top Speed: 105 MPH	4 out of 7
MSRP: $ 1470	

CB500T: 1975-1976

Built for only two years and a truly average model, the CB500T was not highly desired when new or in today's market, making your search for a starting point will be daunting.

By the time 1975 rolled into view, Honda had already earned a reputation for building an amazing array of motorcycles. Numerous formats, displacements and configurations were created as the motorcycle market in the US grew at an amazing and wild pace.

Among their more obvious technical achievements we find a few more commonplace offerings. The CB500T was intended to be an all-around machine that could do a number of tasks well, suiting nearly every need of the average rider. Power came courtesy of a parallel twin, 498cc engine

that produced 42 horsepower. A five-speed gearbox, typical for the period, provided a suitable selection of ratios and a well-padded saddle was comfortable enough for all day use.

Performance of the CB500T was mediocre at best and period reviews spoke of some issues that took points off of a perfect score. When fueled up weight was listed as 463 pounds which was neither horrible nor remarkable and was on par with the rest of the CB500Ts stats. A top speed of just a hint below 100 miles per hour was another notch of average performance in the CB500Ts belt. A disc brake up front and drum on the rear wheel added a hint of safety when compared to other models that carried only drums at both ends.

The twin-cylinder engine was fed air and fuel by a pair of Keihin CV carbs that drank from a 4.2 gallon fuel tank. Each cylinder had its own exhaust tube that swept down from the cylinder head to run along under the crankcase to the muffler in standard fashion. The saddle was 31.5 inches off the tarmac, another fairly average measurement that worked for most riders.

Only in production for two years, the popularity of the inline-four powered models attracted far more interest from buyers as they sought more power from their mounts. 1975 also saw the debut of the Gold Wing which delivered an impressive set of technical advancements, drawing the attention away from anything that was not fitted with as many features.

Year-to-Year Changes

With only a two year production run, the CB500T saw only minor alterations between its debut and disappearance. For 1975 the only color offered was glory brown metallic. The year 1976 saw the return of that hue and was joined by candy antares red. Gold pinstripes were used as accents with both colors in both years as did the brown vinyl that covered the saddle. The faces of the gauges in 1975 were black while green was used on the 1976 editions. No mechanical revisions were listed for the two years and the CB500T was gone as other, more advanced cycles, drew the lion's share of buyers.

CB500T Model Highlights

-    The simplicity of the CB500T creates a motorcycle that can be more easily restored by nearly anyone.

-    The unusual brown seat cover will prove to be a challenge unless you know an upholstery expert who can reproduce the hue and stitching of the original.

-    Unlike many models finding replacement exhaust components is not as challenging.

-    Locating an actual CB500T to restore will also prove to be difficult as they were seldom cherished or retained by the original owners.

-    Having a two year run means that parts from the 1975s can be swapped with those of the 1976 models.

-    A recent search for parts online resulted in a high number of components being offered at a number of locations.

Specifications
Wheelbase: 55.5 in.
Weight: 463 Pounds
Seat Height: 31.5 in.
Displacement: 498cc
Horsepower: 42@8000 RPM
Final Drive: Chain
Fuel Delivery: N/A
Fuel Capacity: 4.2 Gallons
Gearbox: 5-Speed
Top Speed: 99.4 MPH
MSRP: N/A
Production: 1975-1976

Motorcycle Ratings
Available Examples: 2 out of 7
Ease of Restoration: 5 out of 7
Replacement Parts Availability:
*   4 out of 7*
Final Value vs Restoration Cost:
*   2 out of 7*

CB750F Super Sport SOHC 1975-1978

Joining the standard K model in 1975 were the F, or Super Sport editions of the SOHC CB750. The same chassis and powertrain were used on these sportier machines but several alterations were used to differentiate the siblings. As with the K models, changes for each year were subtle and make little difference when it comes to value at purchase or selling time. They were built in far fewer numbers so finding a clean example for your restoration will be a bit more daunting as will replacement parts.

Choosing the F model as your restoration project will result in a tougher time locating correct bits and pieces even if you can find a great starting point machine. Sadly your efforts to return one to its former glory won't guarantee any added value upon completion. Having owned and restored a 1977 F model myself I had fun doing the work but barely broke even upon the sale of my black beauty. A pristine example of the early F models should command a few extra dollars when selling based purely on their lower production numbers, but even then nothing is cast in stone and market fluctuations will take their toll on your asking price.

Year-to-Year Changes

Between its debut for the 1975 model year and the final year of the SOHC edi-

tions, you can see some fairly distinctive changes. The first two years of production saw the tank and tail section finished in a choice of colors with black side covers. The engine cases were delivered in their natural silver trim and a single disc brake was found on the front wheel. Both wheels were of the spoke variety for the first two years.

The four-into-one exhaust was found on the right side of the F model leaving the other flank open for inspection.

The Super Sport editions of the CB750 were clad in unique garb and rolled on Honda's own Comstar wheels in 1977 and 1978.

For the 1977 and 1978 editions of the F model, the engine was finished in black with polished side covers.

This example of a 1978 CB750F has been modified slightly from factory specs but remains a great machine.

Adequately padded for rider and passenger the saddle on the sporty CB750 delivered comfort to spare.

The lower section of the fork legs were also delivered in silver for the '75 and '76 models.

For the 1977 and 1978 models several cosmetic changes were seen. The engine cases and lower fork legs were finished in black with polished covers on the motor. Side covers now matched the chosen unit color. The earlier spoked wheels were supplanted by Honda's new Comstar, five-spoke alloy rims and a second disc brake was found at the front. The four-into-one exhaust was used on all four years of the SOHC F models which saved a bit of weight and added to the sportier aspirations of the Super Sports.

Specifications
Wheelbase: 57.9 in.
Weight: 538 Pounds
Seat Height: 31.9 in.
Displacement in.   736cc
Gearbox: 5-Speed
Final Drive: Chain
Fuel Delivery:(4) 28mm Keihin Carbs
Fuel Capacity: 4.8 Gallons
Horsepower: 67@8500 RPM
Top Speed: 120 MPH
MSRP: $2165 (1975)
Production: 1975-1978

Motorcycle Ratings
Available Examples: 3 out of 7
Ease of Restoration: 4 out of 7
Replacement Parts Availability:
3 out of 7
Final Value vs Restoration Cost:
3 out of 7

GL1000: 1975-1979

The entry of the new Gold Wing to Honda's catalog of offerings for 1975 definitely raised the bar for all touring machines to follow.

The release of the CB750 for 1969 showed the world that Honda was capable of designing and building some truly amazing vehicles. It was only another 5 years before Honda released their newest technological miracle in the GL1000 for 1975. At the heart of the latest model was a 999cc engine with four cylinders in a horizontally opposed format. The smoothness of the new offering was like nothing seen before and the big bike was an instant favorite among cycle fans across the globe.

Unique features were found at every corner of the GL1000 helping to set it apart from any competition of the period. The space that was usually claimed by the fuel tank was actually used for storage with the actual fuel tank placed lower in the frame for better weight distribution. The space within the three panels that opened revealed a tool set and other related bits of hardware for the GL1000. A lengthy wheelbase of 60.6 inches gave the GL a long stride on the open roads and carried five gallons of fuel in the storage tank within the frame rails. Weighing just shy of 650 pounds when fueled the GL was no light weight abut delivered a comfortable ride on the open road. The final drive came via a shaft, versus a drive chain, which added to the silky operation.

Early GLs or Gold Wings were consid-

Designed as a horizontally-opposed four-cylinder the GL1000 engine also raised the bar for smoothness and power.

Finding replacement side covers remains a challenge and plays a big role in the GL1000 design.

The 1976 lineup included the special edition GL1000 that was decked out with gold wheels and unique trim.

ered to be "naked" due to the lack of a fairing and bags at the rear. Later editions would become loaded with protective fairings and methods to carry enough luggage for a multi-day jaunt. The saddle was one of the most comfortable ever seen on a cycle and added to the luxurious ride provided by the GL. A trio of disc brakes helped bring the GL to a halt and spoke wheels were seen on the premier versions of the GL while later versions sported Honda's Comstar wheels.

The humble design of the first Gold Wings has led to nearly 40 years of ongoing assembly, each subsequent year adding more convenience and complexity to the design. All of the upgrades were intended to add comfort and features and spoil the GL rider and a partner. The first GLs carried an MSRP of $2895 in 1975 and the years of new features and power has increased that figure at a rate that kept up with the comfort gained.

Year-to-Year Changes

For the first two years the only change found on the GL was the color of the instrument faces. Dark Green on the debut model and light green on the 1976. For the 1977, '78 and '79 GL the handlebars were taller and a dual level saddle was seen. 1977s also had black gauge faces with green markings.

Found on the 1978 and 1979 models, Honda Comstar wheels replaced the wire spokes, gauges were still black but had red markings. An additional instrument pod was found at the front edge of the faux fuel tank. A revised exhaust was also a part of the '78 and '79 GLs.

Specific to 1979 editions were the rectangular turn signals and a tail light that was borrowed from the CBX with two bulbs and a ribbed face. Control levers were finished in black.

A special edition GL1000 was sold for the 1976 model year, adorned with gold

With rims anodized in gold and gold spokes the Special Edition GL was a one-year option.

Unique graphics were found on the side covers of the Special Edition GL1000.

anodized rims with gold spokes, unique custom candy brown paint and all emblems and striping was gold. A chrome radiator shroud and a leather case for the special tool kit finished off the features of the 1976 Special Edition.

GL1000 Highlights

-    Parts for the early GLs are fairly easy to locate at a variety of sources.

-    As with all of the classic models the exhaust will be the most difficult item to find.

-    Sections of the multi-panel "fuel tank" atop the frame will also pose a challenge if the ones on your restoration project are damaged beyond repair. Side covers can also be listed as hard to find.

-    If you're lucky the wheels and spokes will be in good condition as it can cost $300 per wheel to have them re-chromed.

-    1980 saw the GLs displacement grow by 100cc and the Aspencade and Interstate editions were offered. Both variants were fitted with full coverage fairings, saddle bags and a rear trunk.

-    1984 saw the displacement growing to 1182cc, the bikes were sold in your choice of three trim levels.

-    1988 saw another bump in displacement up to 1520cc along with two additional cylinders.

-    Values for restored or factory original Gold Wings are fairly stable but have yet to climb into an unrealistic bracket.

Specifications
Wheelbase: 60.6 in.
Weight: 647 Pounds
Seat Height: 31.6 in.
Displacement: 999cc
Gearbox: 5-Speed   Final Drive: Shaft
Fuel Delivery: (4) Keihin 32mm CV Carbs
Fuel Capacity: 5 Gallons
Horsepower: 82@7500
Top Speed: 125 MPH   MSRP: $2895
Production: 1975-1979

Motorcycle Ratings
Available Examples: 4 out of 7
Ease of Restoration: 3 out of 7
Replacement Parts Availability:
4 out of 7
Final Value vs Restoration Cost:
3 out of 7

CM185 Twinstar: 1978-1979

The CM185 was a simple machine that could be used for around town jaunts, but was restricted from highway use due to its 58 MPH top speed. Image courtesy of James McCormick

The race to continue building motorcycles with bigger and bigger displacements was often offset by the addition of smaller models at the same time. For the 1979 model year we saw the debut of the massive CBX which set new standards for complexity and performance. In contrast to that newborn bike, the CM185 Twinstar remained on the books. Powered by a tiny 181cc engine that produced only 10 horsepower - nothing could be further from the 1000cc engine found in the frame of the CBX.

The reason for building smaller machines and keeping them in the lineup were numerous. Not every rider was capable or even interested in riding a machine of the CBXs dimensions, leaving room for smaller models. Many buyers were first-timers or simply seeking a method of making short trips around their homes, not travelling across the country.

The basic nature of the CM185 appealed to riders of many stripes in spite of the low power and lack of speed needed to navigate the nation's highways. Weighing only 302 pounds when topped off with all fluids made it an easy choice when riding around town for errands or fun. The four-speed gearbox was another hindrance to some riders but offered more simplicity to others.

The gauge cluster offered plenty of information for the rider. The two-person saddle was adequately comfortable but with only

10 ponies on tap a passenger really slowed down the CM185. When new, you could ride home a brand new CM185 Twinstar for only $1225 making it a painless option for most buyers. In production for only two years with only cosmetic alterations during that run, finding a clean example is not the easiest choice but can be done. The machine pictured here was found on Craigslist and is in original condition with low miles and the factory exhaust still intact and retains the original chrome finish. The asking price was less than the original MSRP and seemed to be a fair price point.

Slowed by a pair of drum brakes meant you'd be sure to stop eventually but panic stops took years off of your life in most cases.

A single pod contained all of the required instruments and kept the operation simple.

Year-to-Year Changes

With only two years of production to its name the CM185 Twinstar didn't offer any vast changes from one year to the next. Unlike most models sold by Honda the CM185 was offered in the same two color choices for both years. Candy antares red or candy sword blue were your options. Stripes found on the fuel tank and side covers of the 1978 editions were white, gold and black with a "Twinstar" decal in white on the side covers. 1979 models used gold pinstripes to accent the red or blue base coat, teamed with a wider red stripe. The "Twinstar" label was now applied in gold to compliment the stripes. No mechanical alterations were made.

CM185 Twinstar Model Highlights

As we have stated time and time again finding a limited production model in factory condition is the best if not the only way to buy one if it can be found at all. With only two years of factory production pristine examples are a rare find. Replacement parts are of equal challenge in locating so be wary when finding an example that's "95% complete." Odds are that last 5% will give you fits of frustration. No common flaws are listed and the simplicity of the design will save you from some issues that are found on machines with bigger motors and added features. If one can be found that remains in original trim you'll be pleased with the great fuel economy and the entertainment provided when riding.

Specifications
Wheelbase: N/A   Weight: 302 Pounds
Seat Height: N/A   Displacement: 181cc
Gearbox: 4-Speed   Final Drive: Chain
Fuel Delivery: (2) 21mm Keihin Carbs
Fuel Capacity: 2.90 Gallons
Horsepower: 10@7500 RPM
Top Speed: 58 MPH   MSRP: $1225
Production: 1978-1979

Motorcycle Ratings
Available Examples: 2 out of 7
Ease of Restoration: 4 out of 7
Replacement Parts Availability: 2 out of 7
Final Value vs Restoration Cost:
2 out of 7

CX500: 1978-1982

The CX500 was eventually offered in five different configurations, part of Honda's attempt to help the bike appeal to a wide variety of buyers.

The CX500 was first seen as a basic cycle powered by a V-twin engine, but the same machine would later be used as the platform for a small touring bike, and a turbocharged model too. 1978 was the debut year for the basic CX500, its transversely mounted 80 degree V-twin motor promised to be smooth and powerful. A shaft drive added to the mix along with some avant gard body work that was unique to the CX.

Early examples of the CX500 lent themselves well to later editions available in custom and deluxe trim. Later still would the Silver Wing and Turbocharged versions which are covered in their own profiles in this book. The first copies of the new CX

were nicely equipped and provided comfortable riding in a mid-sized cycle. Horsepower was rated at 50 and was capable of propelling the CX500 to a top speed of 109 miles per hour. Fully fueled it weighed less than 500 pounds. A leggy wheelbase of 57.3 inches helped in the stability department on the highway.

In the second year of production the base model was joined by a custom and Deluxe version. The CX500C was the custom style and was dressed with pullback bars, a teardrop fuel tank and dual level seat. A freestanding tail light was used in place of the integrated tail section of the base and Deluxe models. The CX500D or

Deluxe wore a stepped seat, a different fuel tank and additional hints of gold in the trim and badges.

For 1980 the base model was removed from the lineup leaving only the Custom and Deluxe versions. The same liquid cooled V-twin was installed in every variation of the CX along with a single disc brake up front and a drum out back. Shaft drive was also a common trait of the three versions. Later in their lives the Custom and Deluxe would appear for one year in the CX650 form along with the GL and turbo models. 1983 would be the final use of the CX platform as other designs proved to be more popular. Some early issues with the cam chain tensioner slowed sales initially but once the error was corrected the $2398 price tag was accepted more easily.

Year-to-Year Changes

For the base model of the CX family only a few slight modifications were seen between the 1978 and '79 models. The small black rim covers seen on the 1978s were removed for 1979 and the control levers were now finished in black anodizing. A rectangular master cylinder was also found on the 1979. Only the CX500 would be seen with silver Comstar wheels as black was used on the Custom and Deluxe styles.

The Custom that was a debut in 1979 listed only one change for 1980 and that was a speedometer that showed an 85 MPH limit. For the 1981 and '82 editions a leading-axle front fork was used in place of the straight-axle seen for 1979 and '80.

For the Deluxe the only change from 1979 to 1980 was also the 85 MPH speedometer which would stay through the 1981 model. For 1981, forks with air adjustability and an equalizer were used.

CX500 Model Highlights

-    Many copies of the first CX500s suffered from a cam chain tension device that failed. When corrected a series of three small punches were made in a triangle pattern on the crankcase to indicate a fix had been done.

-    The CX500C was introduced as the custom or cruiser fad was gaining ground.

-    The CX500D came along for those riders who demanded more fashion but wanted to avoid the more radical Custom design.

-    While not a common sight in the resale market, enough CXs were made to ensure a fair number of them would be around for today's buyer.

-    The CX500TC was the turbo model that arrived in 1982. The bike was far more popular among buyers despite its added cost and complexity.

-    Replacement parts appear to be quite available at online outfitters, making a restoration project an easier task than some others.

-    Current asking prices for the CX series remains fairly low with the exception of the Turbo model.

Specifications
Wheelbase: 57.3 in.   Weight: 487 Lbs.
Seat Height: 31.9 in.
Displacement: 497cc
Horsepower: 50@9000 RPM
Final Drive: Shaft
Fuel Delivery: (2) 35mm Kelhln
Carburetors Fuel Capacity: 4.5 Gallons
Gearbox: 5-Speed
Top Speed: 109 MPH
MSRP: $2398
Production: CX500 1978-1979, CX500C 1979-1982, CX500D 1979-1981

Motorcycle Ratings
Available Examples: 4 out of 7
Ease of Restoration: 3 out of 7
Replacement Parts Availability:
5 out of 7
Final Value vs Restoration Cost:
3 out of 7

CM400E: 1980-1981

The "E" designation tells us this is the basic model in the CM400 family but still a nice all-around machine.

The 1981 model year for Honda included 47 different motorcycles for both on and off-road use. 22 of these machines were designed for road use and they ranged from a 50cc moped to the glamorous GL1100 Gold Wing. In their ongoing efforts to satisfy every faction of two-wheeled enthusiast Honda included four models that were powered by the same 395cc motor.

The CM series claimed 3 of these and they were the CM400T, A and E models. The CB400T was designated the sporty edition and wore different bodywork to set it apart from the CMs. Of the remaining versions the CM400E was the entry level

model for the beginning rider or for someone who didn't want the complexity and cost of other machines. The E carried a price tag that was $400 lower than the A which was fitted with the automatic gearbox.

The E was delivered with spoke wheels at both ends as well as a drum brake on either axle. The instruments included a speedometer limited to 85 miles per hour per government regulations and a second gauge that wore only warning lights with no tachometer in sight. The same 395cc, parallel-twin engine found on the other models still carried 3 valves per cylinder, a two-into-two exhaust and a 5-speed gearbox. The color palette was also simple with black being the only choice for 1980 and 1981 editions.

A low seat height of 29.5 inches was a nice choice for the smaller rider as was the wet weight of 398 pounds. Rated at 43 horsepower the CM400E wasn't a power demon but had enough gumption to get a rider and passenger around town or even out on the open road. The 56.1 inch wheelbase was compact yet stable once under power. A chain provided the final drive and a pair of 30mm Keihin carbs kept the engine fed from the 3.7 gallon fuel tank.

Overall the CM400E was a nice machine capable of doing nearly everything, just not at the highest levels. As far as a great bike to learn on you'd be hard pressed to find anything better suited to that task.

Year-to-Year Changes

The CM400E was another Honda that was only produced for two years with changes between the years being minimal. On the fuel tank the pinstripes of the '80 were orange and red, mated with a "Honda" emblem in white. 1981 saw gold and red stripes with a "Honda" in gold. Art on the side covers also differed with the '80s wearing "CM400E" decal in white and orange and the '81 label was gold to match the art applied to the fuel tank.

For 1981 the bases on the gauges was chrome, as were the housings for the turn signals. The speedometer, the only real instrumentation, remained the same for both years, along with the spoke wheels and drum

brakes at both ends. The MSRP for 1980 was $1498 and $100 higher for the 1981s.

CM400E Model Highlights

-   Offered as a simple machine when new the CM400E still provides the rider with a basic machine with no extra frills or added costs.

-   The parallel-twin engine provides adequate power while remaining simple to repair and plenty of parts still available.

One cost cutting feature on the CM400E is the use of a drum brake at both ends.

The parallel-twin engine in the CM400E is the same 395cc version found in the other CM models.

The graphics on the 1981 models was finished in gold both on the fuel tank and the side covers.

Most of he the graphics on the E were decals - the Honda badge on the fuel tank was a cast item that stood off the surface.

- Every facet of the E edition was designed to be no-frills and restoring one today means fewer searches for odd parts either cosmetic or mechanical.
- The basic nature of the CM400E also means that seldom were they salted away for a rainy day, most were left to ruin or rot.

A well-padded and spacious saddle allowed a rider and passenger to enjoy the simplicity of the CM400E.

Specifications
Wheelbase: 56.1 in.
Weight: 398 Pounds
Seat Height: 29.9 in.
Displacement: 395cc
Horsepower: 43@8500 RPM
Final Drive: Chain
Fuel Delivery: (2) 30mm Keihin Carbs
Fuel Capacity: 3.7 Gallons
Gearbox: 5-Speed
Top Speed: N/A
MSRP: 1980 $1498, 1981 $1598
Production: 1980-1981

Motorcycle Ratings
Available Examples: 2 out of 7
Ease of Restoration: 4 out of 7
Replacement Parts Availability:
3 out of 7
Final Value vs Cost of Restoration:
2 out of 7

Another method of cutting costs was to fit the E with only a speedometer and a four-light gauge in place of a tachometer.

CM400A: 1979-1981

This CM400A from 1981 was discovered in nearly perfect condition so the new owner experienced very few issues during the restoration.

In an effort to appeal to riders who lacked experience with manual shifting or for those who simply preferred not to shift, the CM400A was fitted with a two-speed, automatic gearbox that needed no clutch. The CM400A was just one variant in the CM400 family. It was not the first foray by Honda into the world of automatic gearbox equipped motorcycles. The CB750A Hondamatic was first offered in 1976 and sold for three years.

The CM400A had a production run of three years and did provide many young or new riders a simpler method for getting around on two wheels. The demand, however was never huge and finding one today will require a dedicated search to unearth a CM400A on the open market.

Powered by a parallel twin-cylinder motor that displaced 395cc, the CM400 line included the E, T and C (for Custom) designations. Three valves per cylinder assisted breathing and helped to bring some added energy to the CM. Finding any of these variants today will prove to be a challenge regardless of your wallet's powers. On the whole they were nice machines that delivered enough power to get you around town and even worked on short jaunts on the open highway. Beyond that the diminished output would prove to be too limiting to expand its use. A single disc brake on the

Like most Hondas of the period, the front turn signals were mounted on stalks.

Two-tone paint was used on the 1981 models with two variations listed.

Don't look for a tachometer, the right side gauge was simply a gear indicator.

front wheel was joined by a drum at the rear and was enough to slow the CM400A.

Although limited in its open road capabilities the CM400A still makes a great learning cycle or a great way to get around town. Finding one in great shape will minimize the pain of locating replacement hardware which seems to be scarce. The one featured here is in original condition and handled with care by the current owner.

Year-to-Year Changes

A limited production run of three years allowed for scant changes between the different editions. For 1979 and '80 two colors were offered. Candy presto red or candy holly green were listed and the 1979s had a set of pinstripes in orange and red regardless of which unit color was selected. The

The two-cylinder engine displaced 395cc and featured three valves each along with a pair of 32mm carbs.

A single disc brake was mounted to the front wheel while the rear wheel carried a drum.

A two-level pillion provided the rider and passenger their own perch and offered plenty of comfort.

1979 models also had a 100 MPH speedometer. Stripes on the 1980 models were bright red on the red versions and dark and light green on the green option. A speedometer with only an 85 MPH limit was used on the 1980 and 1981s. During the final year of 1981, the bike could be purchased in two different two-tone options. Candy bourgogne red with red brown metallic was the first and candy sword blue with blue gray metallic was the second. Both sets of paint were highlighted by gold pinstripes.

CM400A Model Highlights
-   As stated earlier, the availability of complete CM400A motorcycles is limited, simply because there weren't that many manufactured and sold during the three year production run.

-   Recent searches for replacement parts revealed very few choices for any segment of the machine.

-   Keeping the simple two-cylinder motor, equipped with two CV carburetors, running smoothly won't provide too much drama due to its very simple design.

-   Overall, finding a CM400A in nearly original condition is about the only way you'll be able to maintain a positive value if selling becomes an option.

Specifications
Wheelbase: N/A
Weight: 412 Pounds
Seat Height: N/A
Displacement: 395cc
Gearbox: 2-speed automatic with torque converter
Final Drive: Chain
Fuel Delivery: (2) 32mm Keihin Carburetors
Fuel Capacity: 2.5 Gallons
Horsepower: 26.8@8000 RPM

Top Speed: 86 MPH
MSRP: $1518
Production: 1979-1981

Motorcycle Ratings
Available Examples: 2 out of 7
Ease of Restoration: 2 out of 7
Replacement Parts Availability: 2 out of 7
Final Value vs Restoration Cost: 2 out of 7

CB400 Hawk Hondamatic: 1978

This example has been accessorized by a passenger "sissy bar" but is otherwise stock.

There was a period in Honda's history that must have been based on the fact that a motorcycle with 400cc of displacement was the perfect path to follow. This is purely speculation but they did seem to produce a large number of models with 400cc in the frame.

The 1978 CB400 Hawk Hondamatic appeared to be the only version of that combination although similar designs would follow shortly. A few years prior to the release of the CB400 edition Honda built a 750cc model that was also fitted with an automatic gearbox. It was only seen for a three year run and the CB400 came to be

on the same year the bigger version went away.

The two-speed gearbox was aimed at beginning riders or to those who couldn't master the typical clutch and shift lever. Honda's 395cc engine was found in the frame of the Hondamatic with 27 horsepower on tap, and chain drive to the rear wheel. The parallel twin engine was fed by a pair of 28mm Keihin carbs and they in turn were supplied with 3.4 gallons of fuel stored in the tank. A seat height of 31.5 inches was not overly low or high and suited a wide variety of riders. When fueled, the Hawk weighed only 403 pounds which again was not exceptional in either direction. A top speed of just over 100 miles per hour was attainable when enough throttle was applied.

Despite the fact that this version of the Hawk was only built for a single year, many components from the later editions will fit this model and allow you to locate parts without too much grief. The CB400 Hawk I and II were seen following this Hondamatic model and the next cycle fitted with the two-speed gearbox was the CM400A in 1979. The 1981 model year would be the final appearance of any Honda powered by a 400cc engine as buyers demanded more power than the twin could deliver.

The 395cc engine used in the Hondamatic was the same as seen on other Honda models of the same displacement.

Designed for the beginning rider the Hondamatic lay-out was simple and useable by anyone with a desire to ride.

Honda's Comstar wheels were far easier to maintain than a set of chrome spokes and looked great too.

Period correct graphics made it hard to miss the fact that this little Honda was shift-less.

Year-to-Year Changes

Being built for only one year there are obviously were no changes. The 1978 CB400A Hawk was offered in two colors for the year, tahitian red or candy sapphire blue being listed. Regardless of the color chosen accent stripes were applied in black and orange and found on the tank and side covers.

1978 Honda CB400A Model Highlights

-    This version of the 395cc Hondamatic was only sold for one year, but was supplanted by a CM400 version the following year.

-    The Hondamatic edition was designed with the beginning rider in mind and the simple design lends itself well to restoration.

-    A high degree of replacement parts can still be found at several online sources.

-    Components required to repair the automatic, two-speed, gearbox are a bit more difficult to track down, but transmission tends to function for years assuming a reasonable level of maintenance.

-    A pair of Honda's Comstar wheels were used at both ends and are far easier to maintain than wire wheels.

-    A two-into-two exhaust was finished in chrome and as with nearly every machine of the period locating a replacement will prove to be a daunting task.

Sold in one of two colors, the stripes remained the same regardless of which hue was selected.

Specifications
Wheelbase: 54.7 in.
Weight: 403 Pounds
Seat Height: 31.5 in.
Displacement: 395cc
Horsepower: 27@7500 RPM
Final Drive: Chain
Fuel Delivery: (2) 28mm Keihin Carburetors
Fuel Capacity: 3.4 Gallons
Gearbox: 2-speed automatic
Top Speed: 105 MPH
MSRP: N/A
Production: 1978

Motorcycle Ratings
Available Examples: 2 out of 7
Ease of Restoration: 4 out of 7
Replacement Parts Availability:
4 out of 7
Final Value vs Restoration Cost:
3 out of 7

Replacing the tachometer, the Hondamatic models had a gear indicator and warning light filling the housing next to the speedometer.

CBX: 1979-1982

The debut year of the CBX showed the world what a motorcycle could be, the big six-shooter was considered a real techno marvel in its day.

Making its first appearance as a 1979 model, the Honda CBX set new standards for technology in the motorcycle universe. Suspended from the upper frame and used as a stressed member the CBX came with an inline six cylinder engine that displaced 1047cc. In charge of feeding the cylinders was a set of six, 28mm Keihin carburetors. A six-into-two exhaust, dipped in chrome, led the fumes to the rear of the chassis.

The inline-six motor was not the only one on the market as Kawasaki was selling their own twist on a six with the KZ1300. The CBX was air-cooled while the KZ used liquid to maintain the correct temperature. The massive CBX had a claimed output of 103

horsepower, which at the time was a feat seldom seen on a street legal machine. That figure was fairly impressive until you consider the 600 pound weight with a full tank of gas. While not a light weight creation, the CBX could still reach a top speed of nearly 140 miles per hour. The shapely fuel tank held just over 5 gallons of fluid but the range was diminished by the power on tap. A five-speed gearbox was included in the mix and did a decent job of always providing the rider with the correct ratio for nearly any situation.

The CBX carried a hefty price tag of $3998, putting it at the top of the price range for Hondas that year. The CBX even cost

Displacing 1047cc and split into six cylinders the engine of the CBX was a complex design that raised the bar for two-wheeled craft.

A pair of circular gauges were joined by a variety of warning lights, providing plenty of input for the rider.

Well-padded and shaped for the comfort of two, the saddle on the CBX provided a nice home for long jaunts.

more than the massive Gold Wing.

Creature comforts abound on the CBX giving the rider and a passenger more than enough reasons to enjoy day-long rides. The two-person saddle is well designed and padded. The cast handlebars reach back to the rider's hands for a natural posture. The molded tail section was a feature found on other Hondas but the two-tone paint was unique to the CBX. Only two colors were offered on the 1979 and '80 CBX with the black accent stripe when your choice was anything other than black. Gold pin striping added a touch of glamour to the brute.

The CBX was introduced in "naked" trim and with more than 100 horsepower. Each

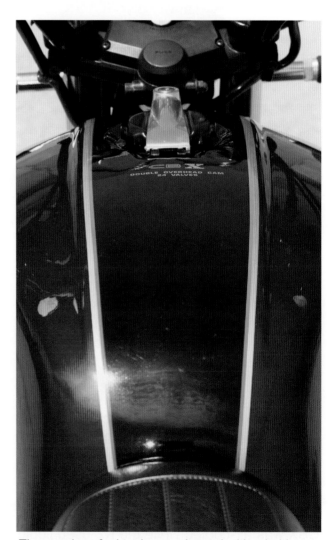

The spacious fuel tank was trimmed with a bold, black stripe on the top along with a set of narrower accent stripes.

subsequent year saw reduced power and added accoutrements. Even losing its dominance in the power division the CBX set the bar higher than most could compete with, and remains a classic today. 1979 models in factory trim claim premium prices over the rest of the years offered and finding one in perfect condition is a rare happening in the current market. If you are lucky enough to own or locate a copy that still has the Honda six-into-two exhaust consider yourself lucky. The fact that you still have that in perfect shape can easily add a few thousand dollars to your asking price.

Year-to-Year Changes

The CBX only enjoyed a four year model run which didn't allow much time for radical annual alterations. The 1979 models rolled on silver Comstar wheels and the bodywork could be bought in perseur silver or candy glory red and either choice came with a wide black accent stripe and gold pinstripes. 103 horsepower was the rating for the first year only. The speedometer showed a top speed of 150, also the only year for that detail. 1980 found black Comstar wheels with silver edging. Colors for the tank and related sheet metal were candy glory red or black. Air adjustable forks and a speedometer that read only 85 MPH accompanied a reduced output to only 98 ponies.

For the 1981 and '82, big changes were seen and felt. Turning the big six towards the sport-touring segment a ¾ fairing was mounted to the frame. The big fairing provided excellent protection from the elements but changed the overall feel of the CBX. A pair of quickly removed saddlebags also joined the fray allowing the rider and a passenger to pack enough for more than one day of riding. An improved Pro-Link suspension was found at the tail end and internally ventilated brake rotors were used up front. The only color sold for 1981 was magnum silver metallic with black and red accent stripes. 1982, the final year of the CBX saw

The matte-black side covers on the 1979 edition of the CBX wore slots and a badge to highlight the mighty six-cylinder beast.

1979 and 1980 models came with this distinctive duck-tail rear section.

Seating position on the CBX gives a nice view of the gauges and warning lights as well as the bold black stripe that runs the length of the fuel tank.

Having lost its naked layout in the previous year the CBX still provided rider and passenger a comfortable mount for long days in the saddle.

A different paint scheme was about all the allowed you to identify the 1982 from the 1981 version, save the alloy grab rail at the rear of the saddle.

an aluminum grab hoop at the rear of the saddle and only one hue in pearl altair white with black and blue stripes. The prominent duck tail seen on the '79 and '80s was also removed from the tail section for the '81 and '82 editions.

The reduced horsepower level introduced in 1980 remained until the end of production. Upgrades in the chassis made a better handling bike for the final two years, but many missed the more powerful debut edition. Thus the value of the first year bikes remains at a higher level than those that followed.

CBX Super Sport Highlights

- As amazing as the CBX is, care must be exercised when taking one home. A high level of mechanical ability is required to do even rudimentary operations. Before the bank of 6 carburetors can be removed for tuning the engine must be unbolted from the frame and lowered to the ground.

- Finding a CBX with a perfect factory exhaust is another daunting task. Finding a replacement unit is harder still and even if found will cost you a substantial bit of scratch. Buyers with foresight took off the factory exhaust when the bike was new and rode using one of a few aftermarket units sold at the time. This allowed time on their new CBX without destroying the six-into-one system.

- Copies of the 1979 edition have retained the highest values due to their higher horsepower

To compensate for the burly bodywork on the '81 and '82 CBX Honda added an upgraded suspension including the Pro-Link system at the rear end.

Honda took the CBX in a different direction for 1981 by adding the large front fairing and matching saddle bags for longer distance jaunts.

rating and the appeal of the naked design. Finding a 1979 in the perseur silver is another wish that seldom comes true.

-   As with the first CB750s , there were a tiny quantity of sand-cast CBXs built. If you are so lucky as to find one, they can be identified by a smaller number of valve cover bolts as compared to later production bikes. The "missing bolts" meant these early editions are prone to leakage from the valve cover. Some of the early bikes also experienced oil leakage of another sort - caused by porous castings.

-   The rabid following of the CBX has resulted in a few great sources for OEM parts and as long as your checkbook has an ample balance you should be able to secure nearly any piece required to bring your CBX back to life. Obviously motor work will not come cheaply either but when well tuned there are only a few machines on earth that sound better at full chat.

-   As with almost every vintage Japanese cycle, finding side covers in mint condition remains a challenge with the CBX. Their construction of molded plastic allows the mounting tabs to break far too easily with few methods of returning them to working order.

-   Upon completion of your CBX restoration you will have a great machine to ride regardless of the miles on your agenda. It was and will always be one of the smoothest running motors ever built and should bring you years of pleasure.

Specifications
Wheelbase: 58.86 in.
Weight: 599.9 pounds
Seat Height: 31.9 in.
Displacement: 1047cc
Gearbox: 5-speed
Final Drive: Chain
Fuel Delivery: (6) Keihin 28mm
Fuel Capacity: 5.28 Gallons
Horsepower: 85.56@9000 RPM
Top Speed: 136 MPH
Production: 1979-1982

Motorcycle Ratings
Available Examples: 5 out of 7
Ease of Restoration: 3 out of 7
Replacement Parts Availability: 4 out of 7
Final Value vs Restoration Cost: 5 out of 7

CB750F: 1979-1982

Replacing the SOHC version for 1979, the CB750F was an instant favorite and is still coveted by riders today.

When the first CB750 made its debut for 1969 the world of two-wheels changed as we knew it. The SOHC design would prevail until the 1979 models rolled into view and reset the bar for performance. The new versions of the CB750 featured a 749cc, inline-four engine that carried a pair of overhead cams which boosted performance and maintained the reputation for smoothness that was set by its predecessor.

The latest entry from Honda was sold in K and F designations, the K being the standard edition with the F once again being the Super Sport iteration of the line. Choosing either variant for your restoration project will be a fine choice based on your preference for either comfort or performance. The K models were built with features that brought

plenty of luxury to the game while still being powered by the newest DOHC motor. The models designated with an F brought performance to the front in both appearance and power.

Supplanting the previous 736cc engine with one that displaced 749cc was the first step, next came the second cam. The F models sported new body work that flowed from stem to stern in one flowing line that ended with a duck-tail rear section that held the tool set provided by Honda. Only two colors were offered for the F model during its four years of production while other cosmetic changes were seen. When filled with fluids the new CB750F weighed in at 542 pounds and was motivated by 65 horsepower at 9500 RPM. A chrome plated four-into-two exhaust kept engine operation quiet while providing an efficient escape route for spent fumes. A bank of four 30mm Keihin carbs delivered fuel to the engine with equal precision. A trio of disc brakes was on duty to slow the new F model down from speed and brought a new measure of confidence to those who rode with an aggressive approach.

The saddle was large enough and came with enough padding to ensure both rider and passenger adequate comfort for long days on the road. Five speeds were included in the gearbox as was typical for the period. Comstar wheels were used on all four years of production of the F model. The MSRP of $2795 was also on target for other machines of the day and seems to be a real bargain when compared to cycles on the market today.

Year-to-Year Changes

The 1979 editions wore Comstar wheels in an all silver motif while the three years to follow would wear black Comstars with silver accents. For the first three years the F models carried engines finished in natural silver while the final year of 1982 sported a blacked-out engine with chrome covers for the clutch, points and valve train. A choice of black or pleiades silver metallic was listed for every year of production with red and orange accent stripes on the 1979 and '82 black Fs. 1980 and '81 editions had only red accent stripes on the dark hue. The silver models wore contrasting stripes of black and red for 1979 and '80 while blue and black were seen on the 1981 and '82 versions. The 1979 editions had a speedometer that listed 150 as the top speed while the remaining years were forced to wear a gauge with an 85 MPH limit. For the 1981 and '82 models the front disc brake rotors were slotted and used dual piston calipers. The front fender was also changed for the last two years and now included a small spoiler on the top curve.

CB750F Model Highlights

- The original popularity of the Super Sport series allows decent examples to be found on today's market although many have experienced trauma.

- Locating a copy still wearing the factory exhaust will again be a challenge, but some buyers were wise enough to baby theirs or remove it for resale later.

- Side covers and the rear tail section can also be found without too much hassle but caution is advised to ensure the items are complete.

- Values of nice originals or restored examples remain in a decent range and if equipped with all the factory hardware a premium will be demanded.

- A myriad of aftermarket exhaust for the F models can also be bought today but will require the carbs to be re-jetted as is true with any exhaust swap.

- Replacing the graphics is the easiest part of the process with OEM duplicates available on at least one website.

Specifications
Wheelbase: 59.8 in.
Weight: 542 Pounds
Seat Height: 31.9 in. Displacement: 749cc Gearbox: 5-Speed
Final Drive: Chain
Fuel Delivery: (4) Keihin VB42B 30mm Carburetors
Fuel Capacity: 5.3 Gallons
Horsepower: 65@9500 RPM
Top Speed: 124 MPH
MSRP: $ 2795 Production: 1979-1982

Motorcycle Ratings
Available Examples: 5 out of 7
Ease of Restoration: 4 out of 7
Replacement Parts Availability: 5 out of 7
Final Value vs Restoration Cost: 4 out of 7

CB650 Custom: 1980-1981

In Honda's ongoing efforts to provide a motorcycle to nearly every segment of the community there have been several versions of their machines through history. We have often times seen K, and F designations applied to the "Standard" and "Super Sport" models and now a new moniker was found. Attaching a "C" to the displacement meant you were riding a "Custom." This designation was typically seen on cycles with a stepped saddle, pullback handlebars and other features unique to that class of machines.

The CB650 Custom was first sold as a 1980 model and had been preceded by more standard issue examples. The Custom label brought two-tone paint, a steeply stepped saddle and handlebars that were a bit higher and reached farther back than those found on the non-Custom models. In addition to the cosmetic alterations the latest C models carried some upgraded hardware as well. The 627cc, inline-four had been seen in the 1979 CB650s and was unchanged for the Custom. A chrome four-into-four exhaust was also found on the C model along with a 5-speed gearbox and chain drive.

The CB650C tipped the scales at 486 pounds when fully fueled and rode on a wheelbase of 57.1 inches. A fairly low seat height of 30.1 inches also played into the role of the Custom design and made it easier to ride for those who lacked height. A reasonable horsepower rating of 63 meant the CB650C was capable of exceeding 100 miles per hour although not by a huge measure. When new the Custom carried a list price of $2648 and was sold through the Honda network of dealers. Your selection of two-tone paint provided a low-key, almost elegant feel to the

Built for only two years the CB650C was never a hot seller, but offered plenty of features without breaking the bank. Image courtesy of GypsieVintageCycle.com

Dressed in your choice of one of a pair of two-tone paint schemes the Custom had an elegant appearance. Image courtesy of GypsieVintageCycle.com

layout in contrast to some that went for a sporty or less subtle approach. Built for only two years means finding a complete example won't be as easy as some others, but riding one will be rewarding once you hit the open road.

For the most part the CB650 Custom did not excel at anything but didn't fail at any task either. Although well-built and capable at many things it sort of fell between the cracks of the bigger machines and those that were more specific in their assignment. If a cycle that is comfortable and easy to enjoy the CB650C should be on your short list. Finding one in terrific condition will save you the grief of searching for parts which are not prevalent on the market today.

The inline-four engine displaced 627cc and was a smooth performer. Image courtesy of GypsieVintageCycle.com

Year-to-Year Changes

Built for only two years you won't see a lot of changes between the two, but those few they made were fairly significant. For the debut year the front fork was of straight axle design with no air adjustment. A solo disc brake was also found on the 1980 version along with a set of Comstar wheels. Cosmetics on the first year saw only two solid colors offered, black or candy muse red with a simple stripe on the fuel tank.

The 1981 editions were fitted with an upgraded front fork that was of the leading axle layout, with air-assist for added comfort and adjustability.

A second disc brake was also added to the front wheel with the drum unit out back. A pair of two-tone color options was listed and

The second model year for the CB650C saw a second disc brake on the front wheel, and an air-assisted fork assembly. Image courtesy of GypsieVintageCycle.com

was applied to the tank and side covers. Candy universal blue with metallic blue or candy muse red with metallic brown were the choices offered.

The price was not altered from one year to the other despite the mechanical and cosmetic enhancements.

CB650C Model Highlights

- Although not an uncommon trait the CB650C was found to suffer from clutch issues. Fixing the flaw isn't tragic but care should be taken prior to riding one home.

- With only a two year production run and a limited audience copies of the CB650C are not a common sight in today's market.

- The example pictured here is a rare treat that retains all of the factory trim and has chrome that still gleams on the OEM exhaust.

- Changes from the first year to the second will force the owner doing the restoration to pay close attention when searching for replacement parts.

- While not as rare as a sand cast 750, the limited production of this machine will hamper your efforts to find a clean copy or the parts to return one to stock trim.

- Values have not responded to the scarcity of the model, based on the fact that when new it wasn't considered a hot commodity.

Specifications
Wheelbase: 57.1 in.
Weight: 485 Pounds
Seat Height: 30.1 in.
Displacement: 627cc
Gearbox: 5-Speed
Final Drive: Chain
Fuel Delivery: (4) 26mm Keihin Carburetors
Fuel Capacity: 3.70 Gallons
Horsepower: 63@9000 RPM
Top Speed: 107.5 MPH
MSRP: $2648
Production: 1980-1981

Motorcycle Ratings
Available Examples: 1 out of 7
Ease of Restoration: 3 out of 7
Replacement Parts Availability: 2 out of 7
Final Value vs Restoration Cost: 2 out of 7

As with any machine of this vintage finding one with the factory exhaust in place and still gleaming is a rare sight and worth a few extra dollars when buying. Image courtesy of GypsieVintageCycle.com

CB 900C: 1980-1982

With a four-into-four exhaust the profile of the CB900C was little changed when viewed from left or right.

It's been more than 30 years ago when Honda first brought their line of motorcycles to the USA. During that period they introduced several designs and concepts that were unheard of prior to the introductions by Honda. Although the "cruiser" classification was not penned by Honda, the popularity of the genre found several versions fitting that mold in Honda's catalogs.

Besting the debut of the CB900F by one model year, the CB900C first appeared as a 1980 Honda. The stepped-saddle, pullback bars and contoured fuel tank all pointed to the "cruiser" designation although it a bit more restrained the others being sold at the time. The inline four-cylinder engine displaced 902cc and exhaled through a four-into-four exhaust finished in gleaming chrome. A trio of disc brakes did an admirable job of hauling the big cruiser down from speed despite its weight of 611 pounds, sans rider.

The most distinguishing feature on the CB900C was the gearbox. It used two shift levers, one to access the 5 primary gears and the other to choose an alternate range effectively giving the machine a 10-speed transmission. The second set of ratios was not a radical departure from gears 1 through 5 but was enough to make a noticeable change. The engine produced 95 horsepower, which for the day was nearing

The CB900C was sold for three years and included a long list of standard features that made it suitable for a myriad of duties.

The dual-range gearbox provided the rider with a 5-speed transmission with a secondary range of ratios that delivered plenty of options regardless of riding conditions.

Fairly typical of the period the CB900C engine was an inline-four design that delivered nearly 100 horsepower.

the upper end of what was being sold elsewhere. A fairly lengthy wheelbase of 62.4 inches and low seat height of 30.7 inches made the big 900 handle like a machine that much smaller. A shaft drive sent power to the rear wheel and added its own measure of smoothness to the overall equation. Comstar wheels were found at both ends and two-tone paint schemes were applied on the 1981 and '82 iterations. A simple instrument cluster told the rider of the basics and was joined by the usual warning lights in case of trouble.

Wearing a price tag of $3498 was not the most expensive bike on the market but was miles from being the least expensive. For the price of admission the CB900C offered a high amount of comfort and features all dressed in an elegant set of sheet metal. Sold for three years, the CB900C may not have dazzled the motorcycle media of the day but having owned one myself I can attest to the overall ease of use and rapid acceleration when the right grip was twisted.

Year-to-Year Changes

In its three years of production the major alterations were found in the cosmetics department with only enhanced brakes for 1982 being added to the roster. For the 1980 and '81 models the engine was finished in its natural silver state with the typical use of chrome covers for the clutch and electrics. The 1980 variants were sold in two colors but each was a monotone design. Candy Muse Red or Candy Poseidon Blue being listed and either came with gold and red pinstripes.

The 1981 CB900C was sold in your choice of two different two-tone schemes. Candy Muse Red was teamed with Brown Metallic or Cosmo Black Metallic was mated to Blue metallic. The two-tone effect was applied on the fuel tank and side covers. One mechanical alteration on the 1981 version was the change to a leading axle fork

A pair of disc brakes at the front wheel were mated to a third on the rear and when used in harmony the CB900C could be brought to a halt with little drama.

The 1981 and 1982 editions of the CB900C wore two-tone paint which was carried over to the side covers.

with air-adjustability on both ends.

1982 found the CB900C fitted with an engine finished in mostly black with valve covers and case covers of silver. The front rotors were now slotted with dual-piston calipers for improved braking power. Colors for the '82s were Candy Muse Red and Candy Antares Red or Candy Empire Blue with Candy Blue to offset the base color.

CB900C Model Highlights

- The CB900C embodies a high degree of comfort and features in a single machine, making it a nice all-around choice.
- The dual-range gearbox was a unique feature that added some fun to your ride even if it wasn't required.

- Locating components online is fairly simple with an extensive array of parts found on a recent search.
- Period reviews of the CB900C were not glowing but few found fault with the big cruiser.
- Locating a project CB900C won't be the toughest part of the process either with numerous examples found on a variety of websites.
- When tuned properly the big CB will deliver an impressive acceleration until you compare it to one of today's available cycles.
- The cost to bring a clean copy of the CB900C won't break the bank and should leave enough cash to repair any issues encountered.

Specifications: 1980-1982 CB900C
Wheelbase: 62.4"   Weight: 611 Pounds
Seat Height: 30.7"
Displacement: 902cc
Gearbox: 10-Speed with Dual
Range 5-Speed
Final Drive: Shaft
Fuel Delivery: (4) 32mm CV Keihin
Carburetors
Fuel Capacity: 4.3 Gallons
Horsepower: 95@9000 RPM

Top Speed: N/A
MSRP: $3598
Production: 1980-1982

Motorcycle Ratings
Available Examples: 4 out of 7
Ease of Restoration: 3 out of 7
Replacement Parts Availability:
4 out of 7
Final Value vs Restoration Cost:
3 out of 7

GL500 Silver Wing: 1981-1982

Honda's CX500 made its first appearance as a 1978 model. The new model was powered by a V-twin engine that was mounted transversely in the frame. Displacing 496cc and mated to a five-speed

When decked out with all of its available storage cases the smaller GL500 Silver Wing Interstate could carry a fair amount of travel gear.

The first year of the GL500 had only a single disc brake on the front wheel while you find a pair on the 1982 versions

gearbox the CX design would be the platform for several other cycles offered by Honda. The turbocharged CX500TC was sold for 1982 only. In non-turbo form the CX500 was sold in base trim for 1978 and 1979 with a Custom variant arriving for the 1979 model year as well. A Deluxe edition was also listed for the 1979 through 1981 model years.

The success of their GL1000 Gold Wing prompted Honda to build a smaller version of the 'Wing - one that would first appear as a 1981 model. The new GL500 Silver Wing and Silver Wing Interstate used the same V-twin motor found in the CX500 series, but added a long list of touring features for added comfort. Other features carried over from the CX line were the 5-speed gearbox, liquid-cooled engine and shaft drive. The base model of the GL500 Silver Wing wore a single disc brake on the front wheel and a drum brake on the rear. The better dressed GL500 Silver Wing Interstates came with a second rotor and caliper on the front.

Both versions of the new GL500 featured a modular seat and trunk configuration that allowed the rider to tailor the GL500 to meet with the specific needs of the ride. There was a dual seat that carried no storage device, a solo saddle with a small rear-mounted trunk and a solo saddle that included a large rear trunk and a backrest. The

Interstate edition was also sold with the three seating options along with a large full coverage frame mounted fairing up front. A pair of removable saddle bags was another added feature found on the Interstate models. A Pro-Link suspension was a part of the GL500 family on the rear end of each bike.

Just as the turbocharged CX650TC arrived for 1983 holding a 674cc engine in its frame, so did the GL650s. A base and Interstate model were once again seen in the catalogs with the same modular seating offered as that seen the year before. The baby GLs were only sold for three years. Bikes built for year one and two were equipped with the 496cc V-twin, while third-year models rolled off the line with the bigger, 674cc motor.

Year-to-Year Changes

Only minor revisions were found between the 1981 and 1982 versions of the GL500 Silver Wings. For 1981 candy muse red or cosmo black metallic were offered while the same red hue was seen alongside the sterling silver metallic in 1982. On the 1982 variants the fuel shutoff valve was vacuum operated and included a reserve position. The same color choices were seen for the Interstate editions as were offered on the base Silver Wing. With the exception of a different set of Comstar wheels and the larger displacement motors of the GL650, Silver Wings built for 1983 used features carried over from the 1982 versions.

GL500 Silver Wing Model Highlights

-   Because the GL series was based largely on the CX models you'll find a high degree of parts commonality for these dressier models.
-   The transverse mounted V-twin engine was a moderately simple design that lent itself well to maintenance when required.
-   The addition of the Pro-Link rear suspension to the GLs delivered a higher degree of comfort especially when loaded for long trips.
-   When searching for either the base GL500 or the added comfort of the Interstate edition take care to make sure every section of the modular seating is still on hand as locating OEM replacements will prove to be a real challenge.
-   Using the engines as a stressed-member of the frame allowed weight to be saved while retaining the chassis' structural rigidity.
-   The larger displacement models of 1983 are a one-year only model making those unique parts tougher items to find.

Specifications
Wheelbase: 58.9 in.
Weight: 518 Pounds
(GL500 Silver Wing)
Seat Height: 30.5 in.
Displacement: 496cc (GL500)
674cc (GL 650)
Gearbox: 5-Speed
Final Drive: Shaft
Fuel Delivery: (2) 34mm Keihin Carburetors
Fuel Capacity: 5.3 Gallons
Horsepower: 50@9000 RPM (GL500)
Top Speed: 95 MPH
MSRP: N/A
Production: 1981-1982 (GL500)
1983 (GL650)

Motorcycle Ratings
Available Examples: 2 out of 7
Ease of Restoration: 2 out of 7
Replacement Parts Availability:
3 out of 7
Final Value vs Restoration Cost:
2 out of 7

CB900F: 1981-1982

When Honda introduced their CB750 for 1969 they not only brought to market one of the best-selling motorcycles of all time but, also created a new segment of the cycle world. The inline, four-cylinder engine became a staple in Honda's lineup as was found in catalogs of every other Japanese maker. Once they witnessed the trend, it was a natural transition to create larger versions of their first SOHC 736cc mill.

The second generation of CB750 was introduced for 1979 and was fitted with a DOHC motor that delivered more power and was also smoother than the previous iteration. It took only a few more years before Honda rolled out the CB900 as a follow-up.

The CB900F cuts a classic profile regardless of which color you select and makes for a great ride.

The 750 variation was still being produced but the 900 offered riders an even bigger slice of the performance pie. The new engine displaced 901cc and was fed by a bank of four Keihin 32mm constant velocity carburetors. This combination produced 95 horsepower at 9000RPM and proved to be a real boon to the freshly minted superbike class. Weighing 578 pounds when topped off, the CB900F was capable of reaching a top speed of 139 MPH.

In its two years of production very little was changed. Both years offered up black with red and orange stripes, or pleiades silver metallic with accent stripes of blue for 1981 and blue and black for the 1982 versions. A chrome four-into-two exhaust bolted to a mostly black engine with silver side and valve covers. Bikes built during both years were equipped with Five-spoke Comstar wheels.

The short production run has left the CB900F in fairly rarified air - a bike that's not easy to find in today's market. Despite that fact prices have yet to escalate into the stratosphere. This is not to say they can be bought

The bold stripe on the tank tells us it's a 1981 edition and the tank holds 5.3 gallons of fuel. 1982 models wore a set of two stripes that flow rearward.

cheaply, but they haven't reached the price levels of some other vintage Hondas.

A comfortable two-person saddle and handlebars that reach back to the rider's hands make the CB900F perfectly capable of being your choice for an all day ride.

As a crossover model the CB900C used the same engine but featured a 5-speed, dual range gearbox that provided 10 rations for the rider to select. A shaft drive was also found on the C or Custom in place of the chain on the 900F. The 900C versions were built for a total of three years starting in 1980 but their production numbers were so low they are another hard-to-find Honda.

Year-to-Year Changes

As stated earlier there were no mechanical or running gear alterations seen between the 1981 and '82 versions. The striping for both base colors changed ever so slightly but beyond that either year would make a terrific addition to your fleet or simply a nice machine to have in the garage.

CB900F Highlights

- As we have learned from other reviews, finding a CB900F with a factory exhaust intact will make for a frustrating search - locating an OEM replacement can be even harder.
- Body panels can be found on a hit and miss basis. As you travel through the search sites I'd suggest you grab any of thc pieces you see as quickly as you can for there may not be another for some time.
- If you are lucky enough to find someone selling one for parts it'll simplify your search.
- A fully restored CB900F might have enough value to ensure you earn back your investment, but once again it all depends on how much you have to spend to bring it back to that shining factory glory.

Slowing the CB900F is the duty of the trio of disc brakes with two up front and the third on the rear wheel.

Displacing 901cc and fed by a bank of (4) 32mm carburetors you'll find plenty of muscle on tap.

The gauge cluster found on the CB900F was typical for Honda at the time.

One of the classic trademarks of Honda's F models was this duck tail rear tail section.

The rear shocks were of the piggyback design which provided extra control and comfort through the adjustments available.

- Prices for clean examples of the CB900F have yet to become obscene and as long as the owner isn't trying to recoup every dime of his investment you can do OK when it comes to buying.

- The Custom version CB900C can be found with a little less searching due to its three-year production. Like the F model, prices for the 900C have yet to rocket northward.

- Returning either model to its former glory will reward you with a fine motorcycle, one that can putt around town, rip down a canyon road, or do light touring with the addition of a windshield and soft bags.

Specifications
Wheelbase: 59.6 in.
Weight: 578 Pounds
Seat Height: 32 in.
Displacement: 901cc
Gearbox: 5-Speed
Final Drive: Chain
Fuel Delivery: (4) Keihin 32mm
Constant Velocity Carbs
Fuel Capacity: 5.3 Gallons
Horsepower: 95@9000 RPM
Top Speed: 139 MPH

MSRP: $3349
Production: 1981-1982

Motorcycle Ratings
Available Examples: 2 out of 7
Ease of Restoration: 3 out of 7
Replacement Parts Availability:
3 out of 7
Final Value vs Restoration Cost:
3 out of 7

MB5: 1982

When Honda first arrived the in the USA they offered motorcycles powered by 49cc engines that were easy and fun to ride. Their goal was to attract riders who may have been hesitant to buy and ride any of the much larger machines being sold. As time rolled on buyers were trending towards cycles powered by ever increasing displacement models, leaving the smaller designs behind. While Honda could see that flow of interest they knew that there would always be buyers who didn't need anything bigger than a 49cc motorcycle.

Combining the small displacement engine with features usually found only on larger machines, the MB5 was created to fill a niche. The MB5 was only sold for one year but did provide owners with a unique set of features that provided a terrific experience despite its smaller size. A pair of 18 inch Comstar wheels and a disc brake on the front wheel were two of the more obvious upgrades to the MB5 when compared to earlier 49cc Hondas.

Once seated you'd find a pair of instruments that included a speedometer and tachometer. A 5-speed gearbox and manual clutch added some big-bike flavor to the mix and the two-stroke engine delivered snappy performance in spite of its limited rating of only 6.3 horsepower. Final drive was via chain and a top speed of more than 50 MPH was listed on the spec sheet.

Weighing only 192 pounds when fueled, the MB5 was handy on the street or in more rural riding situations. A seat height of only 29.5 inches also made it easy for riders with a limited inseam to enjoy the MB5. A single 16mm carburetor was in charge of delivering the fuel to the tiny motor with its reed valve design. A glossy black exhaust led

The smaller size and long list of features made the MB5 a versatile choice for riders of many sizes and disciplines.

The bright 2.4 gallon gas tank helped the MB5 to look good while running for miles and miles between fill ups.

spent fumes away from the chassis. 2.4 gallons of fuel could be stored in the tank providing the rider with a long ride between fill-ups.

Sold in your choice of red with a blue stripe or black with red accent the MB5 looked great no matter which hue was selected. The contours of the bodywork and saddle lent a definite sporting flair to the lay-out.

Year-to-Year Changes

Being sold for only one model year didn't allow time for alterations to be seen on MB5s sold in the states.

A five-speed transmission made it easier for riders to make good use of the 49cc engine's limited output.

MB5 Model Highlights

- The pint-sized MB5 made a great around town choice or pit bike at your local race venue.
- The single cylinder engine and 5-speed gearbox were simple in their design and easy to maintain.
- Online sources for many parts can be found without too much effort while certain components may remain elusive.
- Costs for replacement parts have yet to reach levels of other machines and as long as you aren't starting with a complete basket case you may be able to restore an MB5 without breaking the bank.
- The MB5 provides its owner with a set of advanced features in a compact package that can be utilized in a variety of riding situations.

Specifications
Wheelbase: 47.8 in.
Weight: 192 Pounds
Seat Height: 29.5 in.
Displacement: 49cc
Gearbox: 5-Speed
Final Drive: Chain
Fuel Delivery: (1) 16mm Carburetor, Reed valve
Fuel Capacity: 2.4 Gallons
Horsepower: 6.3@9000 RPM
Top Speed: 50+ MPH
MSRP: N/A
Production: 1982

Motorcycle Ratings
Available Examples: 2 out of 7
Ease of Restoration: 4 out of 7
Replacement Parts Availability: 3 out of 7
Final Value vs Restoration Cost: 4 out of 7

VF750C Magna: 1982-1983

The iconic cruiser design was well represented by Honda's early Magna even though it would only enjoy two years of production.

The latter part of the '70s and into the '80s, the motorcycle industry had developed stronger distinctions between styles of their product. Classifications like Sport, Cruiser and Touring each claimed their own spot in the lineup and offered the rider a specific set of features. The Cruiser or Custom group was obvious due to the split-level saddle, buckhorn handlebars and exaggerated teardrop tank contours. The general layout was meant for comfort for short jaunts with a fuel supply to match.

The first VF750C Magna appeared as a 1982 model and encapsulated the Cruiser style in classic style. A lengthy wheelbase of 65 inches and a low saddle height of 29.9 inches both helped puch the Magna into the cruiser category. Add to those features a fuel tank capable of holding only 3.7 gallons of fuel and the layout was complete. In spite of its custom designation the VF750C produced 79 horsepower and could achieve a top speed of 102 miles per hour. The 748cc motor was linked to a 6-speed gearbox and shaft drive adding some desired smoothness to the blend. A front wheel that was 2" larger than the rear hoop also played into the cruiser configuration and played a role in the handling of any machine in this category.

Topping off the VF750C with fuel pushed the weight to 538 pounds but the general layout carried the center of gravity at a lower point than many thus offsetting the excessive tonnage. The handlebars were higher than most and crved back gently to reach the rider's hands without effort. Instrumentation was basic and was aided by a standard set of warning lights to keep the pilot informed of trouble.

In its original designation the VF750C was only sold for two years but would make a return as a 1988 model that was completely redesigned. The latter Magna would be sold for a single year before returning a third time in 1994. After that introduction the name and model would stay around for a much longer production cycle. Although the first iteration of the Magna didn't stay around long the cruiser classification would remain for decades.

Year-to-Year Changes

The limited production of two years would hamper the changes seen but still there were several to be listed. Colors available for the 1982 VF750C were Candy Maroon or Candy Imperial Blue. Candy Maroon returned for 1983 but was offered against Black as your second hue.

The 1982 Magnas were trapped in the government lunacy of 85 mile per hour speedometer limits while the 1983s were allowed to show 150. The front brake discs of the 1982s wore straight grooves while the second year found curved grooves instead.

Both years were dressed with speedometers, fenders and headlight buckets of chrome as well as side covers that matched the selected paint color found on the fuel tank.

VF750C Model Highlights

- Built to fit into the cruiser mold, the Magna was a comfortable ride around town but as with all machines of that ilk, sometimes played havoc with lower backs.
- Despite the limited riding range the Magna was equipped with plenty of features to make for a great choice when choosing between other machines in the same genre.
- Parts available for your restoration are readily available and can be found on several popular websites.
- Locating a donor cycle may take a bit more effort as when they were new they seldom earned the rating of an icon and were often discarded after use.
- With the motor being liquid cooled extra caution should be taken when shopping for your Magna to avoid examples with mistreated and corroded cooling components that will add untold expense to your restoration.
- The generation of the VF750C that began in 1994 will reward you with a wider selection of machines to start your project as well as additional parts used for that purpose.

Specifications
Wheelbase: 65"
Weight: 538 Pounds
Seat Height: 29.9"
Displacement: 748cc
Gearbox: 6-Speed
Final Drive: Shaft
Fuel Delivery: (4) 32mm Keihin Carburetors
Fuel Capacity: 3.7 Gallons
Horsepower: 79@9500 RPM
Top Speed: 102 MPH
MSRP: N/A
Production: 1982-1983

Motorcycle Ratings
Available Examples: 2 out of 7
Ease of Restoration: 3 out of 7
Replacement Parts Availability: 4 out of 7
Final Value vs Restoration Cost: 3 out of 7

CX500 and 650 Turbo: 1982-1983

The 1982 CX500T was the world's first turbocharged production motorcycle and brought new levels of complexity to the market.

If you have decided that restoring a simple machine from Honda's history is too easy, doing the same on one of their two turbo models will be sure to present enough challenges for almost anyone.

During the latter '70s and early '80s the insurance industry was trying to put a damper on people buying the liter sized cycles from any builder. They were raising insurance premiums on anything bigger than 900cc with hopes of keeping riders on smaller and allegedly safer cycles. In an effort to keep the performance at an appealing level, the big manufacturers of Japanese motorcycles began selling turbocharged models to the public. Honda was

the first to offer a production turbo model and their first foray into the arena was the 1982 CX500T. Powered with a 500cc, twin-cylinder engine that was boosted by a turbo they provided one option for buyers who still sought a high level of performance while dodging the insurance gouging. Soon after the turbo models began to appear the insurance industry did get wise and pounce on them as well.

The CX500T was an amazing machine in its time and remains so today. Sadly not a lot of them were produced making replacement parts a real chore to locate on the current market. There are huge followings for the puffer bikes so finding answers

The Day-Glo trim on the 1982 CX500T was unique and gave the turbo model another reason to stand out from the crowd.

The pearl shell white paint was accented with day-gor red stripes and a pair of gold anodized alloy wheels.

A large, molded section of polycarbonate kept the headlight bulb safe and also added a level of continuous contour to the fairing.

is not an issue, but locating the needed hardware often is.

The debut model was draped in flowing bodywork and finished in pearl altair white and moonstruck silver metallic paint with day-glo red stripes. Accenting that ensemble were a pair of gold-colored alloy rims which helped set the turbo apart from anything else on the road. A comfortable two-person saddle provided the rider and a passenger ample seating for long days on the road.

For 1983 the CX lineup was bumped to 650cc and the turbo edition followed suit. Different colors marked the '83 edition as did the silver alloy rims in place of the golden units of the debut model. Both versions worked well when tuned to factory specs but were intensely complicated in their design and execution. A high degree of computer power was on board although the dependability of that type of brain had yet to earn the level of security we have today.

Valuations on these rare models have yet to climb to expected levels although the popularity hasn't dropped in recent years. The limited production of both the 500 and 650 variants means that parts are very hard to find. Add to that fact the complexity of the running gear and you have a bike that's more difficult to restore than most other Honda models from the same period.

Year-to-Year Changes

-    Each of the Honda turbo models were only produced for a year and any alterations between the 1982 CX500T and 1983 CX650T are largely cosmetic.

-    Displacement was raised from 497cc to 674cc between the two versions with little else altered mechanically.

-    The CX500T was rated at 77 horsepower and the CX650T came with an additional 20 ponies.

-    The 1982 CX500T sports gold alloy rims, bold, day-glo red graphics offset by moonstruck silver metallic panels and a mostly blacked-out engine and exhaust.

- For 1983 the CX650T rode on silver alloy hoops and was trimmed with red and blue graphics on pearl shell white and candy aleutian blue paint.

- MSRP on the 1982 model was $4898 the 1983 model was only one hundred dollars higher.

CX500T and CX650T Model Highlights

- Finding a complete example of either 500 or 650 variants is often frustrating due to the limited production numbers.

- Only 5343 of the 1982s were assembled and of those only 2525 came to the USA. Even fewer of the 1983s were produced meaning the 1983 bikes are even harder to find.

- One fairly problematic feature on both versions was the charging system. The stator and rotor were highly susceptible to failure and difficult and costly to replace.

The gray accents used on the side panels were joined by the nomenclature for the machine.

The surface of the CX500T seat was not the typical vinyl but a kind of semi-textured material that helped the rider stay in his seat when the throttle was twisted.

Adding to the unique nature of the CX500T was the set of gold anodized rims that offset the paint scheme used on the sweeping body panels.

- Both were fuel injected and the 650 version was fitted with improved fuel injection hardware and software to provide better fuel delivery.

- Magazine reviews of the day reported that the acceleration was brutal with very little warning before the boost kicked in, making them a handful to ride for the less experienced rider.

- At 581 pounds wet the turbo models weren't light weights but were certainly not the brawniest machines on the road at the time.

When it returned to the catalog for 1983 the turbo model had gained displacement and power, and was dressed in slightly less dramatic colors

Specifications
Wheelbase: 58.9 in.
Weight: 581 pounds
Seat Height: 31.6 in.
Displacement: CX500T: 497cc
CX650T: 674cc
Gearbox: 5-speed
Final Drive: Shaft
Fuel Delivery: Electronic Fuel Injection
Fuel Capacity: 5.3 Gallons
Horsepower: CX500T: 77
CX650T: 97
Top Speed: 123 MPH
MSRP: CX500T: $4898
CX650T: $4998
Production: 1982, 1983

Motorcycle Ratings
Available Examples: 3 out of 7
Ease of Restoration: 2 out of 7
Replacement Parts Availability: 2 out of 7
Final Value Vs Restoration Cost: 2 out of 7

- The two year production of the turbos from Honda made the bikes very collectible despite their issues with the charging system and low fuel efficiency.

- There is a fervent group of followers for the turbo machines. It's an audience willing to provide direction, but seldom able to provide any of the hard-to-find parts.

- Finding either model in factory condition is rare, but remains the best method available to get aboard an exciting Honda from the early '80s at a fair price.

- Restoring one found in rough condition will be a vastly complicated process as you hunt for needed body parts and mechanical components.

- Sadly, current prices for pristine examples have floundered as owners discovered the limited availability of needed replacement parts.

As on the debut edition, the engine of the CX650T was draped in black with only the polished valve covers for contrast.

VF750S Sabre: 1982-1983

Honda had already earned legendary status as a builder of the inline-four powered motorcycles and in the latter part of the 1970s began to entertain different configurations. Obviously the V-twin design had been around for decades and made famous by several makers both in the US and overseas. So when deciding how to up the ante, Honda chose to add another pair of cylinders.

Once they had determined the best method of creating such an engine they used the basic format in several different models. The 90 degree, V-4 engine was liquid cooled and produced a smooth and powerful output in the mid to upper 80 horsepower range. One model powered by the new motor was the V45 Sabre. The V45 declared the 748cc displacement as well as the layout which was the V-4. The Sabre was a sibling to the Magna and Interceptor, all of which were powered by the same engine with different tuning to suit each model's intentions.

The Sabre was not a compact or lightweight machine with a wheelbase of 61.4 inches and a wet weight of 539 pounds. The 90 degree motor produced 86 horsepower at 9500 RPM and magazine reviews in the day raved of its smoothness and even power delivery at nearly any RPM. A quadrant of 32mm Keihin carbs meted out the fuel at an efficient pace and assisted in the smooth operation of the big V-4 motor. A final shaft drive added to the equation as did the Pro-Link rear suspension. Dual discs were found up front, while a drum did duty at the rear. A five-speed gearbox carried an additional 6th

gear that was considered an overdrive, which allowed the VF750S to run at lower revs at highway speeds. A terminal velocity of 149 miles per hour was attainable with the big Sabre. A saddle height of 30.4 inches gave the machine a lower center of gravity and made it accessible to shorter riders.

The saddle and shape of the handlebar created a comfortable riding posture. The

1983 was the second and final year of production for the 748cc version of the Sabre with the tariff ruling taking effect as of 1984.

With a liquid-cooled V-4 engine, shaft drive and a six-speed gearbox the VF750S Sabre was a complete package that was fast and comfortable.

Sabre provided a comfortable platform for one or two riders. Honda offered a sport fairing and accessories to make the Sabre a great touring mount and allowed riders to custom tune the equipment to their needs. An MSRP of $3398 wasn't a huge bargain but did deliver a high level of equipment for the money.

Year-to-Year Changes

Despite the many talents the VF750S displayed it ended up being produced for only two years. For 1984 the ridiculous tariff kicked in, reducing the Sabre's displacement to only 700cc. The debut year of the V45 Sabre was 1982 and the bike came to the market well equipped. Another governmental regulation decreed a speedometer that showed only 85 MPH as the limit even though everyone knew the machine was capable of exceeding that figure handily. The air cleaner cover was trimmed with a "V-Four" applique that was finished in silver. Each of the disc brake rotors featured grooves of a straight dimension. black or candy bourgogne red were the options for paint for 1982. The 1983 editions of the V45 Sabre featured a speedometer that ran up to 150 MPH, a far more accurate gauge given the potential of the Sabre. Disc brake grooves were curved for 1983 and the applique on the air cleaner cover was black with a white outline. Color options were similar with black or candy wineberry red listed on the spec sheets.

VF750S Sabre Model Highlights

- With only a few notable exceptions, cycles produced in this period and beyond have yet to gain any true collector demand.
- The Sabre was well equipped, powerful and a great handler but still kind of fell through the cracks among the competition, both from other Hondas as well as other manufacturers.
- Locating a suitable copy of the Sabre isn't going to be the hardest segment of the journey as clean examples can still be found without a lot of digging.
- Some early examples of the machine did suffer from premature camshaft wear

which greatly affected performance and longevity of the model.
- Replacement parts are available readily online allowing you to restore a copy of the Sabre without excess digging.
- In keeping with the circa and underlying considerations, the V45 Sabre will probably never reach the cherished strata of a true collectible.
- Whether collectible or not the V45 Sabre will still provide you with years of riding pleasure without worry that added mileage will depress the value.
- Nearly all of the components can be interchanged between the 1982 and 1983 versions, with the exceptions of the disc brake rotors, speedometer and decals on the air cleaner cover.
- The parts CAN be swapped between the two years but are only accurate when applied to the corresponding year of production.
- The use of electronic components as well as more complex assembly stylings make the modern day cycles like the Sabre a bit more of a challenge to restore if major components are missing or damaged.

Specifications
Wheelbase: 61.4 in.
Weight: 539 Pounds
Seat Height: 30.4 in.
Displacement: 748cc
Gearbox: 5-Speed plus overdrive
Final Drive: Shaft
Fuel Delivery: (4) 32mm Keihin Carburetors
Fuel Capacity: 4.8 Gallons
Horsepower: 86@9500 RPM
Top Speed: 149 MSRP: $3398
Production: 1982-1983
Motorcycle Ratings
Available Examples: 3 out of 7
Ease of Restoration: 2 out of 7
Replacement Parts Availability: 5 out of 7
Final Value vs Restoration Cost: 3 out of 7

CB1000C: 1983

1983 would prove to be the final tariff-free year for foreign motorcycle manufacturers, before implementation of the five-year tariff on foreign motorcycles of over 700cc (i.e. non Harleys). The CB1000C was the continuation of the CB900C in many ways but carried additional displacement of its inline-four engine. The CB900C had been on the roster between 1980 and 1982 and did well in the latest "cruiser" class. The "Custom" designation was a close sibling to the cruiser and both terms could be interchanged.

The CB900C had been powered by a 902cc engine while the bigger CB1000C featured 973cc of enhanced power. Coupled to the enlarged motor was the same five-speed, dual-range gearbox. This design provided the rider with 10 different ratios versus the usual 5 or 6 seen elsewhere. The difference between the dual-range ratios was subtle but were considered an important feature at the time. A final shaft drive played a role in the smooth performance available from the big CB1000C as well as eliminating the required chain maintenance. A lengthy wheelbase of 64 inches and low seat height delivered a stable ride at any speed while still being easy to maneuver in parking lots.

Tipping the scales at 608 pounds when fully fueled the CB1000C was not a rocket ship but still delivered 89 horsepower at a lazy 8000 RPM. A top speed of 121 miles per hour

was available with aggressive use of the twist throttle.

The bigger Custom was similar to the 900cc model it replaced, but did have a tail light that was better integrated into the rear chrome fender. A choice of two different two-tone paint schemes added an air of elegance to the biggest Custom with black with

A long wheelbase, low seat height and dual-range gearbox provided riders with plenty of stability and options.

The big Custom featured a tail light that was integrated into the rear fender and helped add to the sleek appearance of the big CB.

Wearing the Black and Achilles Black Metallic paint the CB1000C was an elegant option for those who sought liter-sized comfort.

achilles black metallic the first and candy regal brown with chestnut gold metallic the other. Black and silver Comstar wheels were at both ends along with a blacked-out motor with silver highlights and covers mounted in the middle. A fully chromed four-into-four exhaust was assigned the tasks of keeping things quiet.

Models in the Cruiser bracket from Honda became fewer in numbers in the years that followed as more "naked" or standard models joined the sporty editions. The fabric of the motorcycle buyer was constantly changing and Honda did its best to keep up with tastes that changed like the wind in your hair.

Year-to-Year Changes

The CB1000C was produced in only one year, thus there are no other years with which it can be compared. Although a highly competent machine with loads of features the cruiser class was being replaced by designs that catered to different slices of the buying public.

CB1000C Model Highlights

- With only a single year of production the CB1000C was not a common sight when new and is even harder to find today.

- Remaining examples are found on the occasional search in person or online, with clean copies carrying a slightly higher asking price.

- Replacement parts both minor and major are still seen on the open market with prices that seem to stay at a decent level.

- Unlike some other one-year-only models the CB1000C never drew a large audience despite its stable ride and comfortable features.

- Subsequent models would still be listed under the "cruiser" heading but many riders were drifting towards the ultra-comfort or sport machine arenas.

- The best way to begin a restoration of a CB1000C is to find one in nearly stock condition as locating OEM exhaust and some other major components will provide a challenge.

Specifications
Wheelbase: 64 in.
Weight: 608 Pounds
Seat Height: 31.89 in.
Displacement: 973cc
Gearbox: 5-Speed, Dual-Range
Final Drive: Shaft
Fuel Delivery: (4) 32mm Keihin Carburetors
Fuel Capacity: 4.42 Gallons
Horsepower: 89@8000 RPM
Top Speed: 121 MPH
MSRP: N/A
Production: 1983

Motorcycle Ratings
Available Examples:
2 out of 7
Ease of Restoration:
3 out of 7
Replacement Parts Availability:
3 out of 7
Final Value vs Restoration Cost:
3 out of 7

CB1100F: 1983

Honda's first DOHC, inline-four cylinder engines appeared in 1979 and were installed in the now iconic CB750. As in every segment of the motorcycle world, buyers are always looking for more power. The CB750 was followed by a short run of 900cc models in the CB900 which was then trumped by the CB1100F of 1983 fame. Carrying an engine that displaced 1062cc within the frame gave the latest superbike from Honda a real edge over previous entrants in that category.

Built with an impressive array of features, the CB1100F was loved by magazines of the day as well as riders from across the globe. From the fork-mounted sport fairing to the unique tri-color paint scheme the CB1100F was a distinctive motorcycle; great visual appeal with power and performance to match. Black chrome covered the four-into-two exhaust system, complimenting the blacked-out engine. Rated at 110 horsepower at 8500 RPM it was among the fastest cycles offered for sale in 1983. The low end grunt was one of its more dominant strengths, a trait often noted by magazine reviewers of the day.

Not a light weight machine, the CB1100F proved to be stable at speed, with a well-shaped saddle that made riding comfortable for one or two. A trio of disc brakes dragged the big liter bike down from speed without fuss and the adjustable suspension added to the overall comfort of the biggest inline-four in

Honda's dossier for 1983. A top speed of 144 MPH placed the CB1100F among the top performers of the day. An MSRP of $3698 seems cheap compared to the machines being sold today, but was a tad pricey in 1983.

Loaded with fuel and fluids the 1100 tipped the scales at 586 pounds keeping it

The distinctive sport fairing and contrasting paint scheme help to set the CB1100F apart from Honda's other Super Sport models.

The other color option was the pearl shell white with candy capiolani blue accents

By the 1983 model year Honda had perfected the formula for their inline-four cylinder motor and the 1062cc unit used in the CB1100F was the most potent to date.

The bar mounted fairing was a unique feature to this model and is essential when restoring one back to original condition.

far from the light weight division, but similar in bulk to others in the same class. The 32.3 inch seat height was actually lower to the ground that its predecessor the CB900F due to the bike's smaller diameter rims.

The CB1100F was sold in one of two color schemes. Pearl shell white was either contrasted by candy pearl maui red or candy pearl capiolani blue. This theme was carried from the bikini fairing to the duck-tail tail section regardless of which colors were selected.

Almost in defiance of the one-year CB1100F production run, prices have remained stable over the last several years. Of course if you locate one that remains in factory trim, including the black chrome exhaust, you'll pay a bit more, but even then selling prices have yet to meet with the exclusivity of the model.

Year-to-Year Changes

Once again, the CB1100F was only produced as a 1983 model and was not seen beyond that. Being a one-year-only design tells us there are no changes to be seen.

CB1100F Highlights

-    Though built for only one year, Honda's CB1100F can still be found for sale on a variety web sites, and brick and mortar locations.

-    Prices are stable, not yet reaching the levels you'd expect for such a limited-production, high-performance offering.

-    If staying true to factory form matters, you'll want one that still carries the original four-into-two, black chrome exhaust.

-    Replacement cost for an official Honda exhaust unit, even used, will require nearly a quarter of the value of a restored unit.

-    The factory bikini fairing is another important feature that should be sought when buying your own CB1100F.

Regardless of which colors were selected they were carried seamlessly from fairing to tank and side panels before ending on the tail section.

The sporting nature of the CB1100F was evident, whether viewed from the front or rear.

- Much of the body work and even the graphics can be had without too much grief, eliminating one level of pain from the restoration process.

- A majority of required engine components can also be found without too much effort or expense, save the pesky exhaust assembly.

- Overall, the odds of you making any money by restoring, then selling, a clean CB1100F is a fools bet. Yet, the big 1100 remains a very desirable machine in the eyes of many riders and enthusiasts.

Specifications
Wheelbase: 59.8 in.
Weight: 586 Pounds
Seat Height: 32.3 in.
Displacement: 1062cc
Gearbox: 5-Speed
Final Drive: Chain
Fuel Delivery: (4) 33mm Keihin CV Carburetors
Fuel Capacity: 5.28 Gallons
Horsepower: 110@8500
Top Speed: 144 MPH
MSRP: $3698
Production: 1983

Motorcycle Ratings
Available Examples: 2 out of 7
Ease of Restoration: 3 out of 7
Replacement Parts Availability:
2 out of 7
Final Value vs Restoration Cost:
4 out of 7

VT500 Ascot: 1983-1984

The early part of the 1980s found the two-wheeled market bursting with variety of motorcycles. Finding a machine to fit your very specific needs was easier than ever and Honda played a part in the phenomena by offering a wide variety of cycles to fit nearly any riding style.

Only sold for two years, the VT500 Ascot was the follow-up to the FT500 that had been on the roster for the prior two years. The big difference was that the FT had only a single cylinder engine while the VT carried a twin cylinder mill in its frame. The VT's engine displaced 491cc whereas the FT had been a 498cc. Both designs were designed to appease a wide range of riders and be a good all-around choice for nearly anyone. When topped off with all fluids the VT still weighed less than 500 pounds and the motor produced nearly 50 horsepower. The five-speed gearbox also had a sixth gear that was an overdrive allowing for smoother, low-RPM miles on the highway.

The Ascot was named for a famous racetrack and was styled in a mild flat tracker format. The Shadow of the same period shared many traits of the Ascot but was closer to the "cruiser" layout. A shaft drive was another facet of the Ascot that helped to deliver an easy to ride and maintain machine. The V-twin was in a 52 degree configuration, liquid-cooled with three valves and two spark plugs per cylinder. A flat handlebar played into the racy nature of the design and the narrow saddle did nothing to reduce the effect. A single disc brake up front was mated to a drum at the rear for adequate stopping power. A top speed of 122 miles per hour was attainable if the rider was so inclined.

The ever-changing nature of the cycle market in that period had the VT500 Ascot on sale for only two years. 1983 and '84 were the only chances the V-twin Ascot had to shine and it did so

1984 would be the final year the Ascot was sold while its cruiser sibling, the Shadow, would prevail through 1986.

One feature that illustrates the sporting nature of the VT500 were the lower set of handlebars.

but not in huge numbers as buyers faced a myriad of other choices both from Honda and many others.

Year-to-Year Changes

With only two years of production we once again see very little in the way of differences between the two. Colors for 1983 were listed as pearl siren blue with silver side panel graphics or candy bourgogne red with black side cover accents. The 1984 versions were either black with silver side cover trim or the same red as in 1983 with black side panels. The Honda "Wing" on the fuel tank was finished in two-tone for 1983 and three-tone for 1984. The 1984 models also gained a vacuum operated fuel petcock to better control the flow. Prices for the 1983s was $2498 with the '84s costing $100 less. A black chrome exhaust was standard on both years for the VT500 in contrast to the chrome found on the Shadow variant.

Specifications
Wheelbase: 58.1 in.
Weight: 450 Pounds
Seat Height: 31.7 in.
Displacement: 491cc
Gearbox: 6-Speed (5-speed with Overdrive)
Final Drive: Shaft
Fuel Delivery: (2) 32mm CV Carbs
Fuel Capacity: 3.6 Gallons
Horsepower: 47.5@9000 RPM
Top Speed: 122 MPH
MSRP: $$2498 (1983) $2398 (1984)
Production: 1983-1984

Motorcycle Ratings
Available Examples: 2 out of 7
Ease of Restoration: 4 out of 7
Replacement Part Availability:
5 out of 7
Final Value vs Restoration Cost:
3 out of 7

VT500 Model Highlights

- Clean examples of the VT500 Ascot are not impossible to find, but as is typical of the period be sure that all the factory trim remains in place.

- Replacement parts for these cycles are reasonably accessible on several online sources, making your repair and restoration a bit easier.

- The simple nature of the VT500 design provides the beginner with a machine that can still be disassembled and returned to OEM condition with little drama.

- Upon completion you'll have a great all-around cycle to ride everyday.

- The Cruiser version of the VT500 was sold for four years longer than the Ascot proving the strength of that trend when compared to the versatile VT500.

When you chose to ride a black Ascot home for 1984 the side covers were trimmed in silver.

A solitary disc brake was found on the front Comstar wheel and a drum unit was used on the rear.

VF750F Interceptor: 1983-1984

By the time the 1983 model year came into view, Honda had forged a well-deserved reputation for innovative and dramatic engine designs for their racing and street motorcycles. The debut of the CB750 for 1969 set the stage for inline-four engines but the 1983 models took a different tack.

The "VF" in the name of the new VF750F Interceptor stood for V-Four as their latest power plant chose that path as they attempted to dominate another segment of the market. Although the V-four format had been used in automobiles for decades it was an early appearance in the two-wheeled world. Honda introduced their V-four in the VF750C in 1982 and the Interceptor was the first

The sleek lines of the newest model from Honda were put to good use on the street and tracks across the country in the Superbike category.

sporting application of the fresh design. Liquid cooled and featuring four valves per cylinder the VF750 was a potent performer. Delivering 86 horsepower at 10,000 RPM the new VF750F had a top speed of 134 MPH. The narrow dimensions of the motor aided the aerodynamics of the package as did the frame-mounted factory sport fairing. The rectangular-section, steel perimeter frame also played a part in keeping the machine rigid at speed. A comfortable saddle was all part of the game and provided plenty of comfort whether riding solo or with a partner. The seat height is a bit tall for some riders with a height of just over 32 inches from the pavement.

Despite Honda's prowess in designing engines, the VF750 was plagued at an early age by Camshaft failures. Discovered on both the street going models as well as the race bred versions, this issue held the Interceptor back from being a truly magnificent machine. Once the issue was addressed the Interceptor could be a dependable and highly enjoyable model for riders of nearly every stripe.

The 16 inch front wheel was another recent development that would find its way onto the race

This example wears a replacement front fairing that is missing the striping between the red and white sections of paint but is otherwise all original.

tracks as a way of providing nimble handling due to the smaller diameter and the resulting loss of the gyroscopic effect. Also assisting in greater handling was Honda's TRAC anti-dive braking at the front fork. When the brakes were applied aggressively the TRAC design reduced the dive of the front fork legs thus keeping the cycle better balanced during hard stops. A pair of disc brakes at the front were mated to a third at the rear. When put to use the three disc brakes were capable of stopping the VF750F with no hesitation.

The appearance of the VF750F at Honda dealers caused quite a stir. The bike's success soon led to additional models from Honda powered by similar V-four motors.the Vs-four bikes proved a success for Honda on both the Street and the race track.

Year-to-Year Changes

Only offered for a two year period, changes between the years were minimal and wholly cosmetic. For 1983 the versions wearing the candy aleutian blue paint wore blue stripes while the candy bourgogne red models used red stripes. The "V45" applique on the side panels was black on the red ver-

sions and red on the blue variety. For 1984 the two primary color choices wore stripes of a contrasting hue. Red stripes on blue and black accents on red. The "V45" label was now white with a lack outline to make it stand out on the white background of the side panel regardless of which variant was ridden home. The motors for both years were covered in black as were the exhaust systems. Polished covers for the clutch and ignition offset the otherwise black motif. The visible fins on each cylinder were also highlighted with their natural silver.

VF750F Model Highlights

-   About the only technical glitch of the VF750F were the camshaft failures, the rest of the design was innovative and sound

-   The rectangular-section steel perimeter frame was of stout construction and did a great job of keeping the Interceptor on its true path.

-   The sporting nature of the engine and bodywork lent itself well to those machines sent to the track on both privateer and professional levels of racing.

-   Replacement parts appear to be fairly available at a variety of online sources including body work and sheet metal components.

-   Special steps should be taken to ensure the VF750F you are hoping to buy has had the camshaft issue corrected to avoid heart break and added expense once the title clears.

Specifications
Wheelbase: 58.9 in. Weight: 547 Lbs.
Seat Height: 32.3 in.
Displacement: 748cc
Gearbox: 5-Speed   Final Drive: Chain
Fuel Delivery: (4) 30mm Keihin
Carburetors
Fuel Capacity: 5.02 Gal
Horsepower: 86@ 10.000 RPM
Top Speed: 134 MPH   MSRP: $4398
Production: 1983-1984

Motorcycle Ratings
Available Examples: 3 out of 7
Ease of Restoration: 3 out of 7
Replacement Parts Availability:
4 out of 7
Final Value vs Restoration Cost:
3 out of 7

The VF750F seen here is wearing the proper paint and graphics as evidenced by the blue stripes separating the blue from the white paint.

VF500F Interceptor: 1984-1986

1984 was the debut year for the small Interceptor and it was an immediate success with riders.

Reviewing the long history of Honda's motorcycles, we often find certain models sold only in Europe despite the demands of the US buyers. The European market had been given a VF400F model that was a fan favorite. It wasn't long after that when Honda introduced the VF500F Interceptor to the states. By retaining much of the hardware from the smaller model as well as facets of the existing VF750F the VF500F was well received as soon as its tires hit US soil.

The 90 degree, V-Four motor was similar to that found on the 750 version only smaller in displacement at 498cc. Liquid cooling and four-valves per pot were also carry-overs from its bigger sibling. The same box-section steel frame design was also employed in a slightly smaller stature. Having corrected the earlier issues with the camshaft failures the VF500F was not plagued by any related woes. Output for the reduced VF was rated at 68 horsepower@11500 RPM making it no slouch when the throttle was twisted. The fact that the entire package weighed in 100 pounds lighter than the 750 variant was another vote in its favor. A bank of four, 32mm Keihin carbs fed the engine with accuracy and the four-into-two exhaust was efficient in sending spent fumes on their way.

A familiar sport fairing was joined by a

small chin spoiler making the VF500Fs sporting intentions somewhat more obvious. The compact gauge cluster was concealed under the mid-coverage windscreen.

The rigid frame design was augmented by an array of high tech suspension at both ends. The front forks included an integral fork brace, air-assisted tubes and TRAC anti-dive hardware. A pair of disc brakes was included among the rest of the features. Out back we find the Pro-link system that provided the rider with 4-way adjustable rebound damping to allow for custom settings to meet with conditions. Another disc brake was found there too, along with a rectangular-section swingarm. A six-speed gearbox permitted the rider to stay within the peak horsepower range regardless of the demands placed on the VF500F.

A wheelbase of 56 inches and a saddle height of 31.5 inches allowed even riders of shorter stature to feel at home. The dry weight of only 408 pounds did nothing to dissuade the pilot from enjoying spirited riding at every opportunity. Capable of reaching a terminal velocity of 128 MPH only added temptation to the equation. Wearing a list price for the 1984 issue of $2898, this was a great entry point machine with so much to offer.

Year-to-Year Changes

The first two years of production found the variations between them limited. Wheels for both years were natural silver with a black three-spoke design. For 1986 the entire wheel was finished in black. The saddles and front forks were black with a white front fender for 1984 and 1985. The 1986 versions had red applied to their seats, fork legs and front fenders. The debut year wore one of two color combinations.

Candy alamoana red with black and shasta white was one option with candy aleutian blue with fighting red and shasta white the second. For 1985 the pair of color choices changed to candy alamoana red

The "500" on the side panels was only there for the 1984 versions. It was on the seat for 1985 and not used for the 1986 models.

Displacing 498cc and using a 4-valve, liquid cooled design the engine of the VF500F provided plenty of giddy up.

Black chrome was used to plate the exhaust cannisters and looked great when new, but the systems are hard find today.

The 500 came with twin discs up front, and a fork with TRAC anti-dive technology.

with candy blue and shasta white was one with candy aleutian blue with candy red and shasta white the other. The final year listed only one set of colors, the fighting red with shasta white and candy blue illustrated in the catalog. The 1985 editions had "500" printed on the seat in white.

No mechanical upgrades were made in the three years of production for the VF500F.

VF500F Model Highlights

- With its heritage borrowed from the bigger and smaller models in the family line the VF500F had true sport blood running through its veins.

- The compact design and high-grade specifications makes the VF500F a terrific choice for anyone seeking time on their local track.

- Online resources for parts seemed to be strong with nearly every facet of the hardware available in new and used forms.

- The factory black-chrome exhaust will remain your biggest challenge if it needs to be replaced.

- When new these were highly capable machines and if returned to stock trim you'll enjoy the same performance.

- Whether you bought one new or find one today in factory trim your cost of entry will be about the same.

- Cosmetics were the only variations during the three year production allowing for a higher degree of part swapping.

Specifications
Wheelbase: 56 in. Weight: 443 Pounds
Seat Height: 31.5 in.
Displacement: 498cc Gearbox: 6-Speed
Final Drive: Chain
Fuel Delivery: (4) Keihin 32mm
Carburetors
Fuel Capacity: 4.5 Gallons
Horsepower: 68@11500 RPM

Top Speed: 128 MPH   MSRP: $2898
Production: 1984-1986

Motorcycle Ratings
Available Examples: 3 out of 7
Ease of Restoration: 3 out of 7
Replacement Parts Availability: 5 out of 7
Final Value vs Restoration Cost:
3 out of 7

CB700SC Nighthawk S: 1984-1986

Early in the 1980s a certain motorcycle manufacturer in Milwaukee started to complain that they couldn't compete with Japanese cycles of more than 700cc. In response to their whining the US government placed a tariff on any Japanese cycle of that range. To respond to the ridiculous claim and tariff Honda and every other maker from Japan introduced a line of models powered by 700cc engines. Most of the cycles in that category were simply downsized in displacement leaving every other facet of the machine intact. In an effort to expand their offerings in the new class Honda produced the CB700SC Nighthawk S.

The design was fresh and wasn't based on any other cycle in their catalog. Powered by an inline four-cylinder engine that displaced 696cc, the Nighthawk was also fitted with some features that would set it apart from others in the new 700cc family. A 16 inch wheel was found at either end and a shaft replaced the final drive chain found on many other sport cycles. The "S" in the name referred to the sporty nature of the new model and reviews at the time spoke highly of the approach even though the shaft drive flew in the face of sport bike convention. The overall package of the Nighthawk handled well and the reduced displacement of the motor had a negligible effect on the performance. Even at a displacement of 698cc, the engine was still able to produce 80

horsepower at 10,000 RPM - a fact that made the CB700SC notable in its class. Having six speeds on tap also allowed the rider to stay within the hot zone of the RPM range with ease.

The sheet metal was another unique take in the sport bike realm with its angular lines on the fuel tank and side covers. The

This pair of 1984 Nighthawks are each finished in one of the available hues for that year.

The styling was a bit out of the ordinary for the CB700SC but Honda wanted a design that set it apart from others of the period.

The covers on the velocity stacks and valve covers were finished in silver for 1984 and '85 but were all black on the 1986 editions.

Unlike most cycles built for sport riding the Nighthawks used a shaft for their final drive.

rakish lines were carried over to the handlebar mounted sport fairing as well, completing the design and helping it flow from one end to the other. The engine was nearly a total blackout for the first two years and all hints of silver were missing on the 1986 editions.

When fully fueled the Nighthawk weighed 521 pounds, which was another reason for its quick response to throttle input. The layout reduced the typical shaft effect to a minimum taking nothing away from the sporting nature of the beast.

It was only a few years after the tariff was imposed that business improved for the Milwaukee builder and the tariff was eliminated. The CB700SC was a great performer when new and remains so today. They were made in fairly high numbers so finding a clean example today isn't the hardest of tasks and will be rewarding for those who secure one.

Year-to-Year Changes

The CB700SC Nighthawk is another Honda model that was produced for three years but experienced nothing but cosmetic changes from year to year. For 1984 and '85 the color choices were black and blue or black and red. 1984 saw the colored panels outlined with stripes of the same hue while the 1985 version had a white pinstripe to separate the color from the black. The left leg of the fork was adorned with the Honda TRAC logo for 1985 only, the subsequent years saw left legs finished in all black. The engines of the 1984 and '85 models featured silver accents on the cooling fins, valve covers and side covers on the clutch and electronics side.

For 1986 the colors on the sheet metal were trumped up to black with your choice of candy alamoana red or candy aleutian blue. Those units finished with red panels had accent stripes of orange while the blue versions had a red stripe. The 1986 editions also had motors and all related components

Nestled behind the tinted screen of the sport fairing the rider found a full array of gauges to monitor his or her progress.

The crisp contours of the fuel tank reduced interior volume somewhat but 4.2 gallons could still be stored in its shapely walls.

finished in pure black. The wheels also were finished in an all black motif which added a hint of sinister to the bike.

CB700SC Nighthawk Model Highlights

- Although only produced for three years, production numbers were higher than some others making the odds of finding a clean Nighthawk today a bit easier than you might think.
- With only cosmetic alterations seen during the three year production run, parts can be exchanged from year to year without much drama.
- The factory exhaust was a four-into-two affair and finished in black chrome and as with most cycles, replacements are a rare find.

- Overall, locating fresh components for a CB700SC is not the most difficult challenge as many sources online offer a wide variety of parts.
- Being shaft driven, there is no chain to require maintenance, but care must be taken to ensure the fluid level for the final drive is kept to factory specs.

Specifications
Wheelbase: 59.1 in. Weight: 521 Pounds
Seat Height: 31.3 in.
Displacement: 696cc
Gearbox: 6-Speed
Final Drive: Shaft
Fuel Delivery: (4) Keihin 34mm
Carburetors
Fuel Capacity: 4.2 Gallons
Horsepower: 80@10,000 RPM

Top Speed: 147 MPH   MSRP: $3398
Production: 1984-1986

Motorcycle Ratings
Available Examples: 4 out of 7
Ease of Restoration: 4 out of 7
Replacement Parts Availability:
5 out of 7
Final Value vs Restoration Cost:
3 out of 7

Restorer Interview with Roger Smith

What criteria do you use when selecting a cycle to restore?

I choose bikes that I wanted from the past or those I owned but had to sell when entering the Army during Viet Nam. We find that restoring a bike you really wanted helps eliminate restorers remorse – or the bike that was started to be repaired – but ends up in the corner of the garage.

Here is Roger seated on one his earliest project models, a 1979 Honda CBX restored to perfection - just like the rest of his cycles.

Do you have any favorite places, online or real world, to search for parts?

Vintage Japanese parts are still available but in limited supply. Lately, I have been told repeatedly I that I was buying the last one on the shelf. If you have a bike that you will be restoring in the future, take a few minutes and make a list of parts you absolutely need. Do your best to find them now and it will make it much easier than waiting a few years just to find the shelf is bare.

What aspect of a restoration do you find most challenging?

I like the search for parts. It's like being a Detective as you search for that one needed little part. When you find it online or through a friend, it is very satisfying.

What part of the restoration do you find most rewarding?

The fit of Japanese NOS parts. Unlike some European vintage bikes, Japanese NOS parts typically fit when they arrive at your shop. It's nice to see that part of your new restoration bolt together perfectly, making that section look brand new.

What is a typical length of time to complete a restoration?

We typically decide on a restoration project in late summer. That gives us several months to find a bike before the winter in this part of the U.S. takes over. Then from November through April we can bring the bike back to life taking around six months to roll out the latest project just as Winter is ending.

In 2008 Cycle World Magazine chose our Yamaha Big Bear Scrambler as their restoration award winner at the AMA

Invitational Concourse in Ohio. Their representative was shocked to hear that we spent 30 minutes per spoke polishing and cleaning any irregularities. There's lots of time for restoration when it's five below zero in January!

How much of the process is done by third parties?

We can do everything engine wise down to the crankshafts. We had a Kawasaki H1 that needed new crankshaft seals and we had to send it out to a crankshaft specialty shop in New England. They have the special presses, jigs and other tools to do a perfect job first time.

We also let professionals do frame powder coating, chrome and major painting like gas tanks. Browns Plating can even do some vintage pipes now along with vintage original wheels.

How many restorations have you completed?

We have completed 8 recently. I say "we" because my son-in-law Matt Tate helps whenever he can. There is nothing like having two sets of hands when you are installing an engine, forks or a stubborn set of swing arm bearings on a 1969 Suzuki Titan!. It's also nice to have someone who has skills that you do not, like wiring, or meticulous polishing.

What's your next project machine going to be?

I now try to restore bikes that I can actually use and ride. As an example, that Honda Super 90 we had as teenagers seemed so large and powerful. But now at over six feet and 240 lbs, adult men dwarf the bike - and we wonder how it could have shrunk.

So I look for bikes near 500 cc and full size. I mean a 500 cc café-type bike can still be too small to comfortably ride. Bigger guys will have to go to the 750s of the day for a comfortable post restoration ride.

Any thoughts for a first-timer in the restoration arena?

In my experience, for a first time restorer with some mechanical skills and a selection of Metric tools, I would suggest a two stroke twin because of the simplicity of the engine. Two cylinders, two pistons, two heads and one or two carbs. No valves, springs, guides, camshafts, overhead chains and pushrods to install correctly and set properly. Too many folks have begun a restoration, not realizing how complicated a multi-cylinder four stroke engine is. They get stumped and the bikes are rolled into the back of the garage or shed. Begin simple and move to the more complicated projects down the road a little.

Where To Shop Parts

The purpose of this book is to guide anyone interested in restoring a vintage Honda motorcycle. A book that will guide you through the pitfalls of locating, buying and creating a faithful recreation of an original Honda motorcycle.

This chapter will allow you to review many sources for the needed components and services that you will require when going through the process of restoring your chosen Honda. A separate Source Guide can be found at the end of the book that can be used as a "yellow pages" of resources. Having many years of personal experience messing around with vintage cycles, much of the materials spoken of here are based on my own time spent searching for the items required when rebuilding one of my own Hondas. There are many people in this market who have forgotten more about this process than I will ever know and I always suggest you ask those involved for guidance. By learning from their mistakes you can save yourself tons of time and aggravation during the travails of bringing a classic back to life.

Finding a motorcycle to begin your journey

As with any restoration project you need a donor machine to get started. If you are lucky the perfect machine will already be in your garage, just waiting for your attention. Most of us have a cycle in mind but have yet to begin the search for a nice starting point. Before picking a Honda to restore, consider the availability of parts. If the bike is a rare model and parts are scarce, your job will be that much more difficult. In each listing I've tried do give you an idea as to the parts availability, and any special problems that might show up, for that model.

Doing research for the book I found many Honda motorcycles that enjoy a wealth of available bits and pieces which can be bought easily. Other choices bring nothing but a limited market of new or used parts. This avenue doesn't make the job impossible, but will require countless hours of cruising random websites, swap meets and garage sales for the items you seek. The odds of locating a perfect piece using this method can be entertaining but is obviously not horribly efficient. A note of wisdom might suggest that speed is not a great motivator when beginning this process while patience is key.

Nearly every year and model from Honda's catalog can be found by perusing the available resources. Of course finding one that is local or within your budget can open new avenues of frustration, but with enough digging you'll find one that fits all of your guidelines and will make a great starting point for your restoration project. I am lucky to have a few local dealers who trade in the older machines. Their inventory varies on a daily basis but it's in this ebb and flow that your dream machine may drift into view. By telling the sales staff what you are after they can often use their vast array of sources to locate the cycle you seek while saving you days of wasted time and effort.

Locating the parts you need to complete the project

I am not telling you anything new when I suggest turning to the internet as a source for parts and services. Days of travel and equal amounts of time spent wandering the aisles between purveyors of vintage tin can be replaced with only a few hours at your computer. Anyone with a speedy connection to the web will find sources that would never be found any other way. While word of mouth may lead you to some of the same suppliers, the access gained by searching the web is truly dazzling. You can search for a specific component by merely typing it into any number of search engines and be astounded by the response. Obviously, finding parts for an ultra-rare 1969 Sandcast CB750 will pose more challenges than searching for parts for a more ubiquitous machine, but even then there will be people selling exactly the things you need.

One caveat to be heeded when buying online is the reputation of the seller. Without some sort of guidance as to which vendors can be trusted you can spend all sorts of time and money with little or no actual pieces reaching your door. Sadly, there are many who still seem to enjoy scamming others out of their hard earned cash with no intention of supplying the needed items. Word of mouth is again a great way to qualify a seller of products and services, and should also be taken with a grain of salt as certain transactions may shed the wrong light on an otherwise dependable purveyor of parts.

Of the many online auction sites, Ebay remains the leader in the field and their feedback system ranks high when trying to determine which sellers are worthy of your money and which should be

avoided. The sheer number of players signed up for Ebay's access is truly amazing and seems to grow with every passing day. The fact that you can search the entire planet from the comfort of your home office makes the option of shopping in this arena hard to ignore. There are some who are simply not comfortable or computer savvy enough to utilize this method, but they seem to be dwindling in number as access gets easier and the tools needed to cruise the web get better and better.

While providing you with a worldwide venue there are some who still prefer finding parts in a more traditional fashion. A good old fashioned swap meet allows you to find, assess quality, and even haggle on price for your required hardware. Attending a well prepared swap meet will allow you to review thousands of parts in a single day. Of course you will also need to have a firm grasp of the specific parts you seek, in order to avoid buying a part that fits a 1970 model when you need one for a 1968. Subtle differences can make or break your purchase and again many parts can be

You might get lucky and find the exact part you need among the items spread out on this tarp so bring a sharp eye for detail before swinging your wallet into action.

mislabeled, leading you astray. The labeling may not be done incorrectly to deceive you and may simply be the fault of a poor memory or confusion on the seller's part.

I can recall a time when I was taking one machine apart and the removed parts were left unmarked. Finding them on a lonely shelf months or years later, forced me to tap into my failing memory trying to recall whether it hailed from a 1969 or '73 model. There are some people who can identify nearly any part from a given machine but they are a rare breed and often difficult to contact for access to their immense storage bank of knowledge.

Many of my own trips to well attended swap meets offer one vendor after another with large tarpaulins covered with a vast array of hardware. It's either that or a myriad of plastic milk cartons loaded with various bits and pieces. You have to use a really sharp eye to discern a part that is even close to what you seek. A wise buyer will be armed with an intimate image of the

details that separate one part from another. You can encounter incorrect parts on any online source too so an eye for detail, and honesty on the seller's part, are both required to locate the items you need.

Prices for parts can vary as widely as the quality and scarcity of the hardware itself. Your own budget may determine the limits of what can be spent while other parts may be so few and far between you'll be left with no choice but to fork over a large bit of cash to acquire the item. It is always a good idea to put a spending cap on your project or you can easily surpass the value of the completed machine. For many years now, the values of Japanese cycles have been increasing albeit at a slower pace than other segments of the collector market. Often times a vintage cycle will be restored because it played a vital role in a person's childhood and therefor the costs of the job may be considered non-essential as your dreams outweigh the cost of reaching the goal. Common sense will dictate most of our spending plans but the desire to own a piece from your youth may easily exceed reality. Your friends and family may think you've lost your mind, but you'll know the true value of having something you wanted or lost when you were younger.

This CL175 was an example of swap meet fodder and appears to be complete. Ask the seller for details before handing over your hard-earned cash.

Some General Guidelines for Buying a Used Motorcycle

Once you've decided which of Honda's machines you want to own and restore the next step is to check out the world of used motorcycles, with hopes of finding a really nice example that sells for a great price. Like most of us however, you are most likely to locate all kinds of less than desirable models with price tags that aren't in line with what you see. People can always ask what they want for a vehicle and you can always walk away.

Of course we are often pulled in by the attraction of finding THE cycle we've been seeking. Sometimes we're willing to bite off more than we can chew. perhaps to compensate for an earlier disappointment. While a calm head should dictate what you buy, that rational brain often gets pushed aside by animal instinct. In an effort to steer you clear of some obvious mistakes we'd like you to consider the following aspects.

If you feel confident in your own abilities to detect the major pitfalls, feel free to go alone to explore the possible project machine. If you have questions or have little experience in determining what's a major problem it's highly recommended you bring along an associate with the ability to spot troubles in advance. Unless a seller is trying to pull the wool over your eyes they will usually be happy to have another set of eyes check their machine prior to sale. I would rather have someone with more experience than myself check a cycle out before lugging it home. it's a good way to avoid the negative surprises that suck the joy out of the adventure once you get it home find all the things you missed on the initial inspection.

As obvious as it sounds, make sure the chassis rolls freely. Flat tires will often make this a strenuous chore, but as long as the bike can be rolled you have a better idea that the bearings aren't seized in one or both wheels. While that is not always a deal breaker getting frozen bearings out can be a real task and often times tells you of other troubles that lie within the chassis. Bearings that are truly stuck can also be fixed to the wheels and any attempt at removing them destroys the wheel itself, forcing you to replace the wheel as well. Locating replacement wheels is not impossible, but in the grand scheme of things adds another expense to the bottom line

This swap meet vendor offers a wide variety of seats and fuel tanks for numerous machines. Once again, pay attention to details as a unit for a 1973 might not fit a '75.

and pushes your goal one step further from view. Replacing a damaged hub can be done, but will often create collateral damage to the rim and spokes. Given the resources it is often a better choice to replace the entire wheel assembly for a safer result.

If a cycle has been left exposed in the elements for long it will suffer from a variety of seized components and may be better left for Mother Nature to finish off.

Rust is another fairly serious danger that can go unnoticed. A small amount of surface rust on the steel chassis is seldom an issue and can be detected with the naked eye. Any rust that has eaten away at a major component tells you of serious and long term exposure to water and is usually a good indication that you should look for a different machine. Be sure to check for rust on the swingarm, frame and tubes of the chassis at several locations, not just those that are readily visible. Some crawling around in the muck may be unpleasant but

will save you from even uglier surprises later. Besides rust on the frame, be sure to inspect the exhaust from one end to the other for signs of decay. Odds are if you can see rust on the chassis the exhaust will be deeply affected as well. The undersides of the exhaust pipes will usually suffer the most due to water that settles at the lowest point of the tube. Replacing most of Honda exhaust systems is challenging and if located, typically very expensive. The nature of an exhaust system exposes it to high heat and little protection from the elements. Heat and moisture are two of the main killers of a metal structure so be wary when shopping for a donor.

Nearly any motorcycle that has been unused for decades will have bad seals in the front forks. This will result in you getting very little resistance when moving the forks up and down or no movement at all. Minor resistance tells you the seals are gone but that is a fairly simple change to make. No motion at all suggests another point of seizure and all of the potential complications that come along with it. Finding a replacement fork assembly is easier than locating an exhaust but still another cost added to your budget and another search. The forks should also turn freely from side to side unless the steering head bearings have gone bad or seized. As with the suspension travel, uneven motion

In the event you do need some stinking badges, a swap meet vendor like this might be the answer to your dreams.

says the bearings are bad, no movement suggests the dreaded seizure. Steering head bearings are easy to locate, but if frozen can be a huge process to remove without damage to related components.

Rust and decay inside the fuel tank is almost a guarantee unless the owner has taken care to keep fresh gas within the walls during storage. Even old gas can cause corrosion within the interior of the tank so checking the level of rot is important. There are several sealants on the market that can correct nearly all levels of a rotten fuel tank but even the best of them have their limits. Use a small flashlight to shed some light on the interior of the tank to determine the level of decay you are facing. Once again, finding a replacement tank is not the most difficult task, but will add time and expense to the project.

One of the most costly woes you may encounter will be the engine itself. Making sure it isn't frozen into a solid mass will really make a difference when taking on a restoration. If the cycle still has a kick-start pedal it should allow you to kick the motor through the motion without hesitation. Resistance or no movement of the lever will indicate a motor that is at least temporarily stuck. Sometimes a small amount of moisture within the cylinders will cause the pistons to freeze but by using a small amount of lubricant they can be

returned to normal. Of course this can't be done without gaining access to the cylinders, so any hint of a stuck motor may be enough reason to step away. If no kick start is evident you can use a wrench on the hex head found on the end of the clutch assembly to turn the motor. This will also require you to be able to remove the cover on the clutch to gain access and will depend on the owner's willingness to allow this step to take place. While an obvious nuisance for all parties involved it will save you the buyer a world of hurt if you get the cycle home to find the motor seized beyond recognition. If you are lucky enough to find a cycle in good enough condition that you can hit the starter button and hear it turn over, consider yourself lucky. Don't forget to listen for unusual noises. Some noises are common for an engine that hasn't run for a while but will usually clear within a few seconds of operation. Once again,n having a more experienced friend along for the inspection can be a real boon.

Another method of locating a cycle for your project would be to attend one of many auctions held each year. This CB750 needs nothing but a new owner but not every auction item is as clean.

Assuming the motor starts, check the exhaust to be sure there is no excess oil being sent through the pipes and that pressure at each port is equal. This can be done by simply holding your hand in front of each exhaust tube. The pulsations of the exiting fumes should feel about the same at each tube or there may be trouble with pressures within the cylinders. This is another task that can be checked but requires a few tools and some time that the current owner may not have or offer.

If the motor turns over but fails to start you are faced with a myriad of options and potential problems. The easiest of which would be no fuel in the system and easy to remedy by adding a small amount to the tank. Taking the time to check for other options may be beyond the scope of your skills or the patience of the owner. Checking for spark, fuel flow or any number of related issues can take hours of effort and is usually better saved for the comfort of your own garage after the purchase has been made. If a motor turns over freely but doesn't start, the reason can typically be narrowed down without a huge amount of time and research assuming you have the skills and patience to go through each step carefully eliminating one trouble at a time. As time consuming as this all sounds the trouble it can save you down the line is well worth the effort and will save you from having a nice collection of parts bikes that will never run.

Value Ratings for Completed Restorations

Within the text for each of the Hondas featured in this book, we have provided you with a rough idea of what you may expect to get when selling your completed machine. Sadly, much like the weather here in the Midwest, prices go through an up and down cycle with every passing day. Any values listed here are our best effort at providing some guidance on value but cannot be held as a definitive rating. If there was a way to determine THE price for any given collectible, the person possessing that knowledge would have a stranglehold on the market. As with almost any item being purchased, prices can fluctuate wildly depending on condition, accuracy of restoration and the whims of the climate for certain machines.

We have avoided putting actual monetary figures in this book for several reasons. First of all the market for any col-

A rare display of factory exhaust pipes. Knowing what you need and details of what makes it fit your Honda is crucial when searching for parts online or in person.

lectible changes like the wind, therefor making any printed figures out of date before the book rolls off the presses. It is also fairly easy for a person to review ongoing auctions at Ebay and other sites which tend to be the best way to gauge the current status of pricing. If you choose to use Ebay as a guide be sure to check the "listing ended" section to show what the cycles actually sold for, not just what someone hoped to get paid. Anyone can ask a million dollars, but actual prices are a far more accurate method of taking the pulse of a market. We aren't being vague in an effort to confuse but simply want to avoid woes caused by our own personal input swaying the values.

Obviously certain machines will always be held in higher regard than others but even that doesn't offer any guarantee of the selling price. We have all heard the stories about a buyer who happily pays whatever the seller is asking. Those days seem to have fallen by the wayside however in a tougher economy - but that doesn't mean it can't still happen.

The scarcity of any given Honda will help to determine the asking price, but only in rare cases does that price reflect a true collectible. The first CB750s with sand cast engines remain in that rarified category and probably always will be. Additional examples will never be created so we are forced to deal with the few copies left floating around the world. Other models were popular when new and still draw higher bids on the open market. The CL models from Honda are in this category and still have a huge following, even four decades later. The small CB200s have recently experienced a spike in popularity as conversions to Café racers are all the rage.

As a general rule, try to select and purchase a machine based on your plans to ride, not as an investment. While certain models in Honda's history may carry a higher price tag it's no reason to restore one to turn a profit. By restoring a Honda you wanted in your youth or for some aesthetic reason you will enjoy the restoration process regardless of the end value.

Another reason we've avoided calling one machine more collectible than another is due to the level of personal interest you have in a certain machine. There may have been a Honda in your past that you hated to see go. A machine of that type can easily trump another model that the world deems more valuable. This is after all not a contest, and restoring a motorcycle from your past can be far more rewarding putting that time into something that is hot on the market now. With any luck when bringing a Honda of your dreams back to life you'll be able to avoid the costly temptation of spending far more money than you can ever hope to recoup. Of course this is not wrong and you are free to spend as much on your restoration as you see fit.

Despite the conditions of the market and your own limits we hope you can locate, restore and enjoy riding the Honda that puts a smile on your face. By focussing on the fun rather than potential profit, you will seldom be disappointed with the results. As a hobby, restoring vintage cycles by any maker can be a great way to spend your spare time. Try not to set unrealistic time frames on your project either. While the first 95% of the build may flow like honey it's always the last stretch that can get frustrating as one particular part of the restoration or component eludes your grasp.

Restoring any vintage motorcycle with hopes of earning a profit is not a safe way to make a living. Doing it to return a boyhood dream to life or simply as a hobby makes far more sense. Life offers us enough drudgery; restore a classic Honda for the sheer pleasure of doing so.

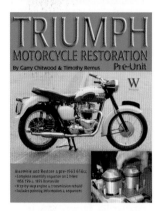

TRIUMPH RESTORATION - PRE-UNIT

Triumph Motorcycle Restoration: Pre-Unit, takes a thorough look at what is required to restore a Triumph 650cc Twin built before 1963. The book is based on two, complete, start-to-finish assemblies, one done on a 1959 model and one on a 1956 Triumph. Each assembly is documented with hundreds of color photographs. Copy includes all necessary details including torque specifications.

The book also includes the complete assembly and overhaul of both the 650cc engine and the four-speed transmission.

Triumph Motorcycle Restoration: Pre-Unit offers the Triumph motorcycle enthusiast 144 pages and over 450 photos explaining how to buy, build and restore a Triumph 650cc twin manufactured before 1963.

Seven Chapters   144 Pages $29.95   Over 450 photos, 100% color

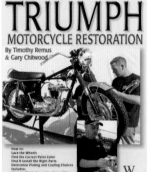

TRIUMPH MOTORCYCLE RESTORATION

As popular as the Triumph Twins were in the 60s and 70s, they are quite possibly more popular now. The new book from Wolfgang Publications offers complete start-to-finish assembly and restoration sequences on two Triumph Twins, a 1963 Bonneville and a 1969 Bonneville. Also included is the start-to-finish assembly of the 1969 engine and transmission. Rather than try to describe the minis-

cule differences that often separated one year from another, this book offers a color gallery with left and right side views of all significant models from 1959 to 1970. With over 450 color photos, Triumph Restoration offers 144 pages of hard-core how-to help for anyone who wants to repair or restore their own Triumph twin.

Seven Chapters   144 Pages $29.95   Over 500 photos, 100% color

HOW TO BUILD A CAFÉ RACER

What's old is new again, and the newest trend on the block is Café Racers.

Written by well-known motorcycle and automotive author Doug Mitchel, How to Build a Café Racer starts with the history lesson. And though those first bikes were build in the UK for racing from café to café, the current rage for Café Racers has definitely spread to the US.

Converting a stock motorcycle to a Café Racer

requires more than a fairing and a few decals. Doug starts the book with a chapter on planning.

The final chapters include two, start-to-finish Café builds. This is the chance for the reader to see how professional shops take a stock Honda, Triumph or Ducati and convert it into a fast, sexy and functional Café Racer, ready to race from café to café on Saturday night, or around the race track on Sunday afternoon.

Nine Chapters   144 Pages $27.95   Over 400 photos, 100% color

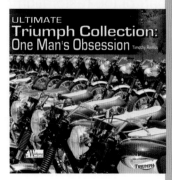

ULTIMATE TRIUMPH COLLECTION

Ultimate Triumph Collection presents nearly 80 perfect Triumphs, from early singles to an immaculate Speed Twin, from an iconic 1953 Blackbird to a pair of 1970 Bonnevilles, all belonging to one man. What started as a restoration project on an old motorcycle twenty years ago grew into a small collection of nice Triumphs.

The meat of this book is the photos of those very bikes, presented one bike per page, each with a short caption. Photos need context; collections aren't built in a vacuum. Chapters one and two provide a histo-

ry of both the collection and the man who built it. Most collections contain a few gems, and those bright diamonds fill the final chapter: The T110 with Swallow side car, the ultra rare 350cc 3H, the '38 Speed Twin, and the new first-year Bonneville.

Ultimate Triumph Collection is an inside look at One Man's Obsession - one man's successful quest to assemble and own the world's best personal collection of the world's most beautiful motorcycles.

10X10 inches, hard cover, printed on art-quality paper. Best selection of Triumphs you'll ever see.

Four Chapters   144 Pages $59.95   Over 300 photos, 100% color   HARDCOVER

Wolfgang Publication Titles

For a current list visit our website at www.wolfpub.com

ILLUSTRATED HISTORY

Ultimate Triumph Collection	$49.95

BIKER BASICS

Custom Bike Building Basics	$24.95
Sportster/Buell Engine Hop-Up Guide	$24.95
Sheet Metal Fabrication Basics	$24.95
How to Fix American T-Twin Motorcycles	$27.95

COMPOSITE GARAGE

Composite Materials Handbook #1	$27.95
Composite Materials Handbook #2	$27.95
Composite Materials Handbook #3	$27.95

HOT ROD BASICS

Hot Rod Wiring	$27.95
How to Chop Tops	$24.95
How to Air Condition Your Hot Rod	$24.95

MOTORCYCLE RESTORATION SERIES

Triumph Restoration - Unit 650cc	$29.95
Triumph MC Restoration Pre-Unit	$29.95

CUSTOM BUILDER SERIES

How to Build A Café Racer	$27.95
Advanced Custom Motorcycle Wiring - Revised	$27.95
How to Build an Old Skool Bobber Sec Ed	$27.95
How To Build The Ultimate V-Twin Motorcycle	$24.95
Advanced Custom Motorcycle Assembly & Fabrication	$27.95
How to Build a Cheap Chopper	$27.95

SHEET METAL

Advanced Sheet Metal Fabrication	$27.95
Ultimate Sheet Metal Fabrication	$24.95
Sheet Metal Bible	$29.95

AIR SKOOL SKILLS

Airbrush Bible	$29.95
How Airbrushes Work	$24.95

PAINT EXPERT

How To Airbrush, Pinstripe & Goldleaf	$27.95
Kosmoski's New Kustom Painting Secrets	$27.95
Pro Pinstripe Techniques	$27.95
Advanced Pinstripe Art	$27.95

TATTOO U Series

Into The Skin The Ultimate Tattoo Sourcebook	$34.95
Tattoo Sketch Book	$32.95
American Tattoos	$27.95
Advanced Tattoo Art	$27.95
Tattoo Bible Book One	$27.95
Tattoo Bible Book Two	$27.95
Tattoo Bible Book Three	$27.95

NOTEWORTHY

American Police Motorcycles - Revised	$24.95

LIFESTYLE

Bean're — Motorcycle Nomad	$18.95
George The Painter	$18.95
The Colorful World of Tattoo Models	$34.95

Sources

www.bikebandit.com

www.cmnsl.com

www.ebay.com

www.hondarestoration.com

www.oldbikebarn.com

www.powersportspro.com

www.randakks.com

www.vintagehondamotorcycleparts.com

www.westernhillshonda.com